Her Name is Missy

A remarkable story of love and terror during an African Ebola epidemic

Gail Gillespie-Fox

With

Graham Spence

Dedications

To Missy and each and every chimp orphaned by man – I wrote this book for you. I hope it helps to curb and most importantly one day soon, end the senseless killing of your wonderful kind.

The tragedy that chimps are now on the endangered list is sad enough, but what statistics don't reveal is the sad and often horrific story each orphaned chimp would tell if they could. With the dismal statistics and current ongoing dwindling numbers, every chimp's life matters.

This book is dedicated to all of those who risk and devote their lives for all creatures great and small.

I have changed a few names to protect identities. This book is a recollection to the best of my memory.

Cover photo: Michael Jedig Jensen

Interior photos: Michael Jedig Jensen, Phoebe McKinney, Gail Gillespie Fox, Mark Fox, and Emily Tarr.

Website: www.barkavenuecards.com

Foreword

GAIL FIRST CONTACTED ME in 2015 asking whether I could help her with a project. She had read Babylon's Ark, a book I had co-written with my brother-in-law, the late, great conservationist Lawrence Anthony, about rescuing the war-ravaged zoo in Baghdad.

Ironically, I was in New York at the time writing a book on a woman who had allegedly been attacked by an iconic Hollywood comedian.

I say 'ironic' as I had just spent the day interviewing people about the baser aspects of human nature and wholesale celebrity abuse of power.

The night the email from Gail arrived. It was the complete flipside of the coin – showing human nature at its most noble.

She was apologetic, she said, about drawing an analogy between the book she was writing, and the work I had done with Lawrence.

In Babylon's Ark many animals were rescued. She had only rescued one.

That immediately struck a chord with me. Babylon's Ark was a grandiose mission, but only for those insane enough to barge into a war zone, such as Lawrence.

Lawrence was gloriously eccentric and relished doing things anyone else considered impossible. He wasn't called the Indiana Jones of conservation for nothing.

But most of us don't get those opportunities, or understandably, are reluctant to take them on.

However, while it is true that Lawrence saved an entire zoo and Gail saved a single tragically orphaned chimpanzee in Liberia, the analogies are still remarkably similar.

For a start, in Iraq, the menacing backdrop was the aftermath of an invasion and a precursor to a looming civil war.

In Liberia, it was the fear and loathing of a country in the deadly grip of a particularly nasty and usually fatal virus called Ebola.

Gail's quest to rescue a tiny chimpanzee called Missy in a time of death and ignorance is, to me, exactly what roots conservation is all about.

It's about ordinary people who have the courage, the will and the iron determination never to give up.

They are, increasingly, the real unsung heroes in combating the growing crimes against our planet. And crimes against our planet, our only home, are to me tantamount to crimes against humanity.

Among the most pernicious threats to modern conservation, as Gail discovered, is bureaucratic indifference.

Sure, there are other conservation issues in the developing world, such as the legacy of eating bushmeat, the hunters who target endangered species, abject poverty, and of course the desperate daily struggle for survival that most of us in the First World have no idea of.

But the real issue is the lack of iron political will to make a change that will actually make a difference.

Few politicians show they have that will. So it is up to ordinary citizens to fill the gap.

Gail has that courage and steel. In spades. That's what struck a chord with me. And that's what made me assist her with this book.

If each one of us has the grit, determination and granite stubbornness that she showed in saving one orphaned chimpanzee that saw its mother being slaughtered for bushmeat, this planet will be a better place for all who inhabit it.

This book is about such people. Ordinary folk stepping up to the plate and saying, 'enough!'

It's also a story about making a difference, no matter how small. For anyone who believes otherwise, perhaps they should take a trip to West Africa and see where Missy, the baby chimpanzee, is now.

Against almost insurmountable odds, she is alive today, thanks to Gail and others like her.

In short, this book is about saving our fellow creatures, even if we have to do so one at a time. I urge you to read it and take courage.

Graham Spence, Author of The Elephant Whisperer, England, October 2016.

One

THERE WERE TWO OF THEM, an old man and a boy. Backlit by the haze that drifted in shards through the thick jungle canopy, they looked almost identical; both as wiry as fencing poles, limbs knotted with stringy sinew sheathed in fascia tissue far steelier than any bulk you could accrue in an expensive gym.

The old man was not really an old man, but he looked wizened and ancient after a hard life in the rainforests of Liberia. He had been born under a mahogany tree and been hunting the jungle for bush meat or fishing the rivers for catfish before he learnt to speak coherently.

He had no doubt that he would be buried beneath a mahogany tree, maybe even the same one he was born under. The rainforest that he called home was all he wanted or asked out of life.

The boy was not really a boy, more of a young man, but in the old man's eyes, he would always be a boy until he learnt the lore of the forest. The old man admitted that the boy had potential, but was still years away from being a master hunter as he, the old man, was.

The old man carried a firearm, a 12-gauge shotgun, that was so worn that you could not read the manufacturer's name etched on the barrel. Archaic as it might be, in the old man's hands it was still a lethal weapon, lovingly cared for and greased with oil from the palms that grew so lushly in the jungle.

With that gun, the old man had shot almost every species of animal in the jungles that hugged Liberia like an exquisite green rug. He had killed a lowland gorilla in one epic encounter, although the old man usually retreated as stealthily as a leopard when he came across the gentle giants that could weigh up to 700lbs. He had not seen a gorilla for years.

He had killed a pygmy hippopotamus, although it was also years since he had last seen that animal. Maybe it was gone for good in this area. Just like the black colobus monkey, another animal he had killed countless times, they seemed to have disappeared. He had shot pangolins - too many to recall, as well as every type of antelope that ran free and wild in the bountiful paradise that seemed to stretch for ever.

But the old man now knew that paradise no longer stretched forever. With the logging companies ripping out the lifeblood of the forests, he could now cover more terrain in a single morning than he could in days of travel just a few years previously. There were sprawling networks of dirt highways slashing deeper and deeper into the jungle to accommodate the 18-wheeler rigs, growling and slipping in the ochre-red mud as they hauled the chopped hardwoods – teak, mahogany, ironwood, okoume – from the continent's lung.

The roads meant that hunters no longer had to hack their way through the dense undergrowth as the animals retreated further. The incessant coughing of the chainsaws and choking diesel fumes from the trucks may frighten the animals, but now it was far easier to go deep into the bush to find them.

And kill them.

Also, with more and more logging crews coming into the bush as they systematically gutted a once virgin Eden, there was an exponentially growing market for bushmeat.

Indeed, as a young man not many years ago, he had harvested bushmeat solely as a subsistence hunter. Animal flesh fed his family and only if there was any to spare would he give cuts to neighbors in his village.

Today his wife owned a rickety store made from palm fronds slashed with a machete which kept the sun off a hewn mahogany log where she sold quartered chunks of everything from bonobo to crocodile. The situation was now reversed; they ate what they could not sell. He was, by Liberian standards, a rich man. But then again, he was the best tracker in the village. Except he was now a commercial hunter, not a subsistence one.

For him, the jungle was the heaven the white missionaries talked about that you only got to experience when you died. The difference was that he experienced it every day. It provided wood for his hut, meat for his family, water to wash and drink and there was no ailment he could think of which the roots and berries that sprouted after the rainy season could not salve.

He instinctively knew the logging companies threatened his paradise, but was also bemused by his new wealth. His wife said some of the bushmeat she smoked even went to Europe, flown out in jets to the hundreds of thousands of expatriate West Africans living in cities with names like London, New York or Paris.

He was not sure whether he believed that, but when one thought that his father had hunted elephant that had once roamed in their thousands in these same jungles just a few decades ago, anything was possible.

The young man did not carry a gun. He had one at home, an old flintlock that had been crafted by a village blacksmith, but it only fired a single lead ball and was not accurate so the old man refused permission to bring it. Instead the younger hunter carried a machete and dozens of wire snares.

That was how they caught the majority of animals – in traps. Shooting was effective, but you first had to find the animals. With snares, the old man could read the bush trails like an encyclopedia and lay traps accordingly, cunningly surrounding the noose with foliage to force a duiker or bongo or bushbuck in the right direction until the noose tightened like a garrote around its neck.

It also meant that he did not have to use bullets. Snares could be made from vines, of which the forest again provided, or wire which he cut from rusting fences in nearby villages. He checked the snares every two days to make sure no other hunter stole his catches.

A slight rustle in a kapok tree caught his eye. He motioned to the boy to stay still.

Then he saw them; chimpanzees in the branches. There were about eight of them.

Chimps were prize bushmeat. His wife would smoke them to give the flesh a rich, earthy flavor. It was a delicacy; strong and gamey and not insipid like the bloodless fare the city people ate.

The chimps were moving westwards, travelling in the lower branches of the kapok, which is one of the tallest trees in the forest. They had not seen the two humans.

The old man and the boy crouched as still as lizards. The wind was blowing just right, coming straight at them. If they waited a little longer the chimps may come down lower for an even easier shot.

They did.

The old man sighted his gun at one of the closest adults. It was a female and now easily in range of his lethal scatter of buckshot pellets. He squeezed the trigger as gently as a caress.

The blast shattered the buzz of the jungle and as the echo died there was absolute stillness. Even the cicadas were mute. The old man and the boy watched the chimp start to tumble out of the tree, almost in slow motion. It was clutching something in one arm and grabbing branches with its other in a futile bid to break its fall.

It thudded to the ground.

The other chimps started screeching, trying to source the attack. With the second barrel, the old man fired at another, scoring a direct hit as it too toppled out of the tree. The old man knew that chimps were ferocious fighters – not as terrifying as the gorillas of course, but they were immensely powerful for their size. They would sometimes bolt if they thought the threat insurmountable. But the old man knew from experience that a troop of chimpanzees often fought to the death to protect their families.

Thus the second shot was fired not only to double his tally, but also to deter the rest of the troop coming to defend their fallen colleague. He suspected that the way the first chimp fell it had been clutching a baby.

He reloaded both barrels of his shotgun and waited for a minute.

The screeching of the traumatized troop quietened as they fled, swinging on branches deeper into the forest. The old man stood up. As he approached the first chimp it suddenly sprang up and came at him, teeth bared and eyes blazing with madness and rage. Half its side was a shattered, bloody mess and but it still moved with incredible speed despite its critical wounds. He fired from the hip. He would not miss from that range.

The chimp's face exploded in a cloud of red mist as it was blown backwards. It did not get up.

The old man walked to the second chimp. He prodded it with the gun barrel. It did not move.

Not bad – two chimpanzees with three shots. He would get good money for that.

The boy called his name. He turned around to see the youngster holding a small bundle. That was why the female had been coming at him with such insane courage and fury. That was why she did not try and escape but instead had charged him. She had a baby. Judging by its size it was just a few days old.

The boy made a motion with his hands as if to wring the infant's neck. The old man curtly stopped him. There was not enough meat on the baby to be of significance. But he had heard that people from the cities like Monrovia sometimes bought baby chimpanzees for pets. The white people in particular were really soft touches ... the baby would be worth much more alive. In fact, maybe even more than the bush meat.

* * *

WE WILL NEVER KNOW exactly how Missy was orphaned, and what I have just described here is how thousands of chimpanzees meet their fate in the rainforests of Liberia.

The slaughter continues each day. But one thing we do know is that she almost certainly would have seen up close her mother being murdered for bushmeat.

Perhaps an aunt and an uncle as well; maybe even the entire troop. It would have happened right in front of her. Chimpanzees love their children as deeply as we humans love ours and will fight with heroic determination to protect them.

There is no doubt Missy would have been traumatized to the edge of sanity, tethered in a tiny makeshift cage or box without her mother and family as she was taken to the towns to be sold.

But how did I, a white South African from the First World city of Johannesburg get involved in all of this?

How did I, taking what I thought would be a hedonistic sabbatical to be with my fiancé in West Africa, end up fighting for a single baby chimpanzee's life?

How did I find the will to take on impenetrable bureaucracy and an Ebola epidemic to try and get a happy ending to a desperately tragic tale of ignorance and, in my opinion, criminal indifference?

It's a long story ... but for me there is only one explanation.

It was destiny.

Two

LOOKING BACK, THE INCREDIBLE adventure kicked off in January, 2013, when my fiancé Mark Fox was offered a three-year contract to work in Liberia.

The contract was straightforward; to implement a distribution network and marketing strategies for a cellphone company.

However, as any Africa hand will tell you, nothing is ever straightforward, particularly in West Africa. Little did we know that this journey would change our lives. And by how much.

Almost prophetically, the contract came about in an extremely challenging – to put it blandly – point in our lives. About two years earlier, Mark had lost almost everything he owned. A deceitful business partner had embezzled funds out of Mark's company and when the dirty deed was exposed, the partner fled to Australia. The betrayal was absolute.

As the partner was untouchable in Australia, Mark had to close his business down without being able to salvage anything. His life's work literally went swirling down the drain.

Then, still reeling from that treachery, he was viciously assaulted and robbed by armed men during a nasty home invasion.

The bandits entered the house in the middle of the night while the family was asleep. They did so by the simple expedient of using the front door key, and even the dimmest Sherlock Holmes could figure out how that happened. The house was being renovated by a construction company at the time, so it was highly likely that the thieves were either some of workers themselves, or at the very least, in cahoots with them.

Mark heard the door opening and confronted them as they came in. There were four; two carrying handguns and two with machetes, or pangas as we call them in South Africa.

Mark courageously tried to take them on, but unarmed and outnumbered, he was soon overpowered. It was not exactly a fair fight. His face was smashed in with a pistol.

The gangsters tied Mark up, his face streaming blood, as well as his wife at the time, Anne.

They then dragged their two terrified children, eight-year-old Sydney Rose and six-year-old David, into the room.

For a dreadful three hours, Mark, Anne and their two small children were locked in the main bedroom while the robbers ransacked their home. It's difficult to imagine the anguish that Mark went through, wondering if his family was going to be harmed, raped or killed, and the sheer helplessness of being tied-up and not able to do anything to protect them. He would have fought to the death to protect his family. Of that, there is no doubt.

The evil thugs took everything of value, flat-screen TVs, computers, and all jewelry, including Mark's prized collection of top brand watches such as Rolex and Breitling. They loaded the stolen goods into a pick-up truck and Mark's car, and left.

It was a slick, well-planned operation.

Then to add to Mark's woes, the insurance company didn't pay him out for his massive loss.

The reason? The alarm was not activated at the time of the robbery. There was no acknowledgement whatsoever that this was almost certainly an inside job way beyond Mark's control. They refused any compensation.

With the collapse of the business thanks to his embezzling partner, the banks then pounced on Mark and repossessed his cars and house. As far as his already rocky marriage was concerned, losing the family home was the final nail hammered into the coffin.

Mark was destitute, but refused to be a victim of circumstances. His resilience is like steel; he doesn't know the meaning of the words 'give up'. His mother is exactly the same, an incredibly determined and wise woman.

So after these setback, which would have crippled many people, he turned to his mother for advice when he got two simultaneous job offers while piecing his shattered life together. Both were from mobile phone companies.

The more lucrative offer was in South Africa, the powerhouse of the continent.

The other was in Liberia, one of the poorest countries in the world.

At this stage Mark and I had been dating for a few months and regularly chatted about our yearning to travel through Africa and other exotic places. So should he take the job offering more money and security? Or the job offering more adventure?

His mother swayed the day. The most logical decision would be to take the more lucrative contract in his home country. But both Mark and his mother think outside the box.

So Mark's mom reminded him that the corporate world of his previous life had been pretty shallow. And what did he have to show for it?

Not much. He had been robbed of everything he owned, either by evil gangsters or an equally evil crook in the guise of being a business partner. The huge sacrifices he had made to get to the top were perhaps just too much, she said. The rewards were too superficial.

In short, taking the job in South Africa may be a case of more of the same. Her advice was that life is not all about money; time is our most valuable asset. I strongly agree with her.

18

My advice to Mark was simpler; just follow your gut instinct. And so he did.

He chose Liberia.

I must confess that even though I urged Mark to act instinctively rather than cerebrally, I was initially not exactly ecstatic at the idea of him heading off into the unknown. And heading off to Liberia gives new meaning to the word 'unknown' for people from the First World.

The country has one of the most blood-soaked histories in Africa, which sadly is no mean achievement on this continent that I love. Indeed, just typing 'Liberia' into your computer's search engine is enough to give you Google gooseflesh.

Top results bring up scores of gory videos and blood-curdling articles about a true Heart of Darkness that makes Joseph Conrad's African novel of the same name look like pleasant bedtime reading. The country had fought two particularly nasty civil wars between 1986 and 2003, and images of cold-eyed child soldiers brandishing AK 47s and graphic descriptions of every atrocity you could think of were recurring themes of a nightmare from which the country has only recently emerged.

Among the more Satanic characters in the brutal conflict was a man bizarrely named General Butt Naked. The self-appointed general, so-called due to his penchant for going into battle without a stitch of clothing apart from his boots, is accused – among much else – of child sacrifice and cannibalism. He has admitted to the deaths of up to 20,000 civilians.

However, Africa being Africa, General Butt Naked whose real name is Joshua Milton Blahyi is now a preacher in Liberia, claiming to have seen the error of his ways and undergoing a Damascene conversion to Christianity.

As you can imagine, this is not quite what you would expect to find on an average Trip Advisor evaluation of a country you were planning to live in for a few years. But being the eternal optimist, Mark instead looked upon his new job as an opportunity; a fresh adventure and foreign places to explore.

That's just the type of guy he is. He had been a soldier in the South African Defense Force (SADF) as at the time it was mandatory for all young white men in the country to do two years' military training.

Soon after being drafted, Mark was selected for the Assault Pioneer Unit, which specialized in small arms and explosives and setting up observations posts deep within enemy territory.

Between 1986 and 1988, he was at the frontline of the fighting in the Angolan civil war among the MPLA, the Marxist government's army, and UNITA (National Union of the Total Independence of Angola) rebels, led by the now deceased Jonas Savimbi, The Cold War was in full swing and South Africa and the West supported Savimbi, while Cuba and the Soviet bloc supported the MPLA.

Mark was far behind enemy lines observing troop movements when, unbeknown to him, his unit was suddenly replaced by another one. It was an impromptu decision taken by the military high command a thousand kilometers away.

They had to move quickly. But his unit commander was unable to raise him on radio and tell him to return to base right away as Mark's battery had shorted.

Also, a few days earlier, while being transported to the Red Zone behind enemy lines, Mark's team buddy had come down with malaria. Mark decided to go on alone.

Without a working radio, there was no way for his brothers-in-arms to let him know they were moving out. Consequently, Mark was oblivious to all the drama. In fact, he was not worried at all about the lack of communications as he knew exactly where he was and would return on schedule.

His commander had no option but to obey orders and leave his man out there in enemy territory – breaking the most sacred ethos of the warrior code.

When Mark returned to base camp a couple of days later, it was completely deserted. Now alone in a red-hot combat zone, he realized his only option was to continue heading south as fast as he could in the hope of catching up with his unit.

Thanks to his broken radio, he was also unaware that the replacement unit, the 81st Brigade, had set up new base camp reasonably close nearby. Otherwise he could have headed there for relative safety.

It's an incredible story. Surrounded by tens of thousands of Cuban and Angolan soldiers, Mark somehow managed to sneak away from under the enemy's nose towards the Namibian border, at least 500 kilometers away. If he had been captured, his treatment would have been brutal.

While he was struggling to get home through the most hostile circumstances imaginable, all his poor mother was told by the South African army was that her son was 'missing in action'.

After two weeks he finally reached a friendly military base on the Caprivi Strip of Namibia, which was called South West Africa at the time and governed by South Africa. It was an amazing feat of guts, endurance and survival, and one can image the absolute relief of his family when they heard he was safe.

In short, he is an exceptionally capable person. Few other people could have done what he did in Angola and survived, so I knew that if anyone could look after themselves in a struggling third world country like Liberia, it would be Mark.

Sure enough, he settled down quickly in the capital Monrovia and as he was enjoying his new home away from home, he asked me to join him for a holiday.

We had actually planned for this. The idea was that one of us would commute every three months so we could spend quality time together, either in South Africa or Liberia. We didn't want to be apart for too long and I was thrilled to know that I would be sharing Mark's adventure.

But even so, I was a little apprehensive as to how much of an adventure it would be. 'Adventure' is a loose word, ranging from something pleasant and exciting to downright terrifying.

And believe me, for a white South African girl from Johannesburg, Liberia was going to be at the very least 'adventurous'.

So I had absolutely no idea what I would be letting myself in for.

However, Mark didn't want this only to be a short vacation together. He wanted me to come up for at least six months, maybe more, so I decided to use the lengthy break as a long-overdue sabbatical from work.

I had been running my own dog grooming business for 18 years with hardly any time off and now my body was weary. Having your own business can be taxing, and I had been running on reserves, if not empty, for too long.

So Liberia wasn't just going to be a holiday; I was instead going to take a deep plunge into the unknown in every sense of the word.

It was a bold move on my part, giving up my pleasant life and my business. However, with the approval of those near and dear to me and my intuition urging me to join Mark, I knew instinctively that it was a risk worth taking.

Although Mark and I hadn't been dating for that long at the time, we had some history, having gone to the same high school together. He was the stereotyped extrovert sporty kid at school, somewhat mischievous, down to Earth, bit of a Mr. Cool, but not a smoothie.

On the other end of the spectrum was me; shy and not comfortable in the limelight. I far preferred being under the radar.

We initially met doing gymnastics, a sport I loved but sadly had to give up when I grew too tall to do it as well as I wanted to. Consequently, when Mark contacted me on Facebook after all these years (25, I shall confess), I was surprised that he remembered who I was.

After that initial reunion thanks to social media, we regularly chatted on Facebook and this eventually led to meeting up in person for coffee. Getting together was great and it didn't take me long to realize just how much I enjoyed his invigorating company. We got on fabulously and our friendship provided a healthy foundation for romance.

Soon we were spending as much of our free time together as we could, which for me was almost unheard of. Indeed, after a few failed relationships, I thought I was destined to be alone.

This was due to two reasons; I invariably felt smothered by spending too much of my time with any 'significant other', but also because my precious Shih Tzu dog called Ming was my priority. The few men I dated didn't understand my devotion to her and unsurprisingly things did not work out. What guy wants to play second fiddle to a fluffy dog?

So now to find myself actually wanting to be with someone else all the time was a revelation.

It just felt so right. Ming had passed away a year before, just missing her 15th birthday. But even so, I knew Mark would never have felt threatened by my commitment to her.

Now that I was off to Liberia, I handed over my grooming business to my sister Sandra, which was tantamount to giving away a piece of my heart. The beloved doggies I cared for and their wonderful owners who started off as clients had now became my extended family.

My sister has the same passion for animals as I do. Knowing that the dogs I had grown to love would be in her caring hands and that I would get regular updates on their well-being, made letting go of the business that much easier.

In fact, the only 'problem' was that Sandra is my identical twin which seriously confused the customers and I think some of the dogs may have wondered why I suddenly smelled different.

Soon it was time to go. Off to West Africa.

It was a bitter-sweet farewell for me. On one hand I was dying to see Mark, but on the other, it was really difficult to say goodbye to my sister and her two children.

Like many twins, we are exceptionally close. We were in the same class throughout school and shared the same extramural activities. We studied together once we had left school, and even after she married, we have never been apart for more than a couple of weeks. Until now.

We said goodbye wiping away tears and with a lump in our throats.

"I promise to phone every second day," I sniffed as the international departure doors at the O.R Tambo airport swallowed me up.

Three

M Y FIRST CONTACT WITH LIBERIANS, a delightful nation, was at the Kotoka International Airport in Accra, Ghana, where I was catching the connecting flight to Monrovia.

I was a couple of hours early and headed for the departures hall which was almost deserted. You would not exactly call it a lounge; more like a bleak room with cheap seating. Not many people were going to Liberia, it seemed.

I chose a seat in an empty row of plastic chairs. Soon after I sat down, a couple came and plonked themselves right next to me despite the many other vacant chairs nearby. It was only around 7 a.m. but they had already opened a bottle of beer. The woman had a fashionable weave and a freshly made-up face, while the man was tall and skinny, wearing jeans and a buttoned shirt.

"Yo' goin' Liberi'?" she asked.

"Yes."

"Okay we sit wid yo'? Firs' time we be on de airplan'."

"This is the first time I've been to Liberia," I answered vaguely. "I'm sure it's all going to be easy going from now on."

I looked away, but she had decided to attach herself to me and continued chatting in her distinctive Liberian accent which initially sounded nothing like English to me. It's a type of musical pidgin vernacular, unique to the country and at first very difficult to grasp. This was my first taste of the land where I would be living in for the next few months. This friendly approach – maybe too friendly for me at the time – was also an indication of the welcoming nature of most Liberians.

When the boarding gate opened and we headed towards the plane, she was still yakking away amiably, while I nodded every now and again without a clue of what was being said.

I found a seat on the half-empty aircraft, and she and her husband or boyfriend once again sat right next to me, despite the many vacant rows.

By the time we landed at the Roberts International Airport two hours later, she had told me her life story. Or maybe not. Sadly, I hardly understood a word of Liberian English, despite this early baptism of fire.

The airport, named after Liberia's first President Joseph Jenkins Roberts and some 56 kilometers outside the

Liberian capital Monrovia, was just as I imagined it would be. A small, run-down building in an open field where the 3,400m landing strip is only big enough to handle smaller commercial aircraft. The stifling heat was a reality check that I had truly arrived in tropical West Africa and was now at the start of a new chapter. I hoped it was going to be an exciting one.

The airport was just as unimpressive inside. The arrivals hall was a drab room with tattered and torn advertising posters stuck on the peeling paint of the walls.

I joined the queue waiting to get passports stamped, not knowing what was coming next.

Unbeknown to me, Mark had somehow managed to wangle his way into the customs area where the public are strictly barred. I certainly was not expecting this and did not see him at the end of the counter, even as I stood there looking straight at him.

Then I heard his voice. It was the best sound in the world.

"Hello Crocodile."

That was his nickname for me. It comes from our way of saying goodbye: "See you later, Alligator," followed by "In a while, Crocodile.".

Well, that's my story. He tells people it's because I snap at him all the time!

With Mark, I now felt safe.

"Hello Foxy-Indy," I replied. That was my new nickname for him. Being an adventurous spirit, I sometimes called him 'Indy' after Indiana Jones and sometimes 'Foxy', from his surname, Fox. I liked the combination of both names because it really summed him up. He is both an adventurer and clever at the same time.

I hugged him tightly and we kissed. "I am so happy to see you. How did you get into customs?"

Mark winked, "This is Africa, Crocodile."

He grabbed my arm and steered me out of the terminal to the parking area where he introduced me to Peter, our driver. Peter, who even at that stage seemed unflappable, politely greeted me and packed my bags into the trunk.

Then we were off to the residential compound where Mark lived, just over an hour's drive from the airport.

Peter was about 45-years-old. He had six children, which is not unusual in Liberia where big families are the norm despite the high mortality rate. He walked with a limp as his one leg was slightly shorter than the other, and took great pride in his job. In fact, at every opportunity, he reminded us that he had once worked as a driver for the Red Cross.

The car's air conditioner was a massive refuge from the stifling tropical heat. As Peter drove off, Mark, who always has an almost encyclopedic interest in everything around him, had read up loads of stuff on Liberia and gave me a fascinating account of the country and its history.

30

The story of Liberia is unique, an often noble saga of struggle, strength, survival – and sadly, savagery. The word means 'Land of the Free' and was named by American slaves that had been set free and repatriated to Africa in 1822. They are known as Americo-Liberians, and are generally lighter skinned than native Liberians. The first Americo-Liberians were mainly devout Christians, while the indigenous people, of which there are 16 distinct tribes, followed more traditional practices, including witchcraft.

For 163 years, Americo-Liberians held tightly to all reins of political power and lived well, even though they only accounted for five per cent of the population. In stark contrast, native Liberians didn't have it that good, even though at one stage Liberia was the richest country in West Africa. 'Land of the Free' didn't hold true with most citizens living in poverty.

This all changed, but not for the better, in 1980 when Sergeant Samuel Doe seized power in a vicious coup d'état and executed scores of Americo-Liberians.

Most of the powerful old families fled to America, while Doe's brutal reign and nepotism of his own tribe, the Krahn, led to the first civil war.

This was soon followed by the second one and the country then plunged into complete anarchy. The war ended in 2003 after some of the most depraved blood shedding and violence Africa, let alone the world, has seen. Recovery is slow. Sadly, Liberia is still among the 10 poorest countries in the world.

The first few kilometers out of the airport were on a 'Highway' that was little more than a two lane tar strip, one in each direction. There were palm trees sporadically jutting out among some houses and buildings, but the countryside was mainly virgin grassland.

We drove over a bridge spanning a magnificent lagoon, which are familiar sights in Liberia. Wide, intriguing expanses of water, studded with palms and mangroves with giant roots reflecting on the surface, the lagoons are like mirages only a million times more beautiful. But that is often misleading. There is abundant natural water in Liberia, but the paradox is that much of it is polluted by mountains of toxic garbage. Most Liberians bathe in wash buckets outside their homes with water drawn from artesian wells.

The scenery started to change as we got closer to the city. The traffic grew exponentially busier and more chaotic. The tropical grassland thinned and was replaced by thousands of matchbox homes, small concrete buildings in desperate need of paint and restoration with tiny windows, which were usually broken. These drab structures were squashed together, threatening to spill onto the road. There was seldom any sidewalk to speak of.

I also couldn't help noticing how many churches there were – although these were certainly not ornate cathedrals. Most were just like any other building we passed; square, concrete and derelict, but with a cross.

The neighbourhood backyards were just sand and muddy pools, even though this was the dry season. The puddles were a magnet for mosquitoes and explained why malaria was such a rampant problem. There was no grass. Not one blade.

The roads were absolute anarchy, and as I am a nervous motorist at the best of times, I was very happy we had Peter with us. Liberians also drive on the right hand side of the road, the opposite to South Africa, so I would've been a wreck trying to steer a car in this country.

As we approached Monrovia, traffic started to jam up like a queue at a rock concert. Motorists forced their way into any space they could find, and soon two lane roads morphed into four barely defined lanes of tightly-squeezed mayhem. Each car seemed to be on the verge of bumping into the next, yet scooters carrying up to four people miraculously managed to weave their way through almost non-existent gaps.

Taxis, which were predominantly yellow sedans, all bore the dings and dents of darting in and out of the chronic congestion, while many were mechanical miracles on wheels in managing to ferry so many passengers.

Peter drove cautiously and confidently, yet also was not averse to contributing to the loud honking. In fact, in Liberia, a horn is considered as essential on the roads as brakes.

The view seldom changed; row upon row of dirty run-down homes with litter strewn everywhere and roads clogged with honking traffic. There were, however, a few newer – I use that word loosely – buildings on Monrovia's main road. They stuck out like roses among thorns.

In the middle of this bedlam, Peter turned left onto a bumpy sand road and then took another left into Ocean View, the name of the compound that was to be my new home.

My heart sank. I was not expecting to live so close to what at times looked little more than an urban squatter camp. This was certainly no leafy suburb.

Welcome to Liberia.

Four

M UCH TO MY RELIEF, IT WAS a very different picture once the 15-foot steel security gates to Ocean View opened and we drove in.

Peter steered down the paved driveway to our apartment. There were two rows of buildings running parallel to each other, all two-stories high and all painted white.

Parked on both sides of the driveway were predominantly United Nations vehicles, the U.N. still being a big influence in Liberia. Even though the civil war had ended 10 years ago, the country was in desperate need of aid.

Most of the other cars were 4x4s, essential to cope with the pot holes and slippery mud roads throughout the country.

At the far end of the complex, a big inviting swimming pool with sparkling clear water beckoned. Adjacent to it, a worn-out but still intact chain-link fence cemented into a concrete base provided a security barrier preventing random access from the beach. The sea with small creaming surf breakers was barely 50 meters away.

In fact, apart from barbed wire jutting out of the top of the perimeter walls to deter intruders, Ocean View looked more like a cluster of modest holiday units than a residential complex. Although it needed a little attention, it had a certain charm about it. Mark told me that this was the most popular in the country and we were very lucky to have got an apartment here.

My apprehension started to ease slightly. I had to admit it was rather beautiful.

Peter carried my bags into the apartment and introduced me to Annie our house cleaner. I liked her immediately.

Annie in turn introduced herself. "Hello Gaal," is what it sounded like. "Mark tol' us all 'bout yo'. He ver' happy to have yo' here. So r' we."

Once again, this was English I could barely decipher, so Mark repeated her kind words. As I discovered on the flight over, most Liberians speak English with a mixture of what I would describe as a half-American, half-Jamaican accent, dropping the last couple of syllables with many words. This makes it hard to understand at first. The double-vowels in my name seemed particularly difficult for them to get their tongues around. Hence 'Gaal' instead of 'Gail'.

With Annie's help, I unpacked most of my clothes. She was about 38 and we were soon chatting freely. She told me about her family and her two sons, one of 16 and the other who was six.

Annie had seen much hardship in her life. Her husband, who like Peter had also worked as a Red Cross driver, was killed in a car crash some years ago when another vehicle smashed into him. The force of the impact had rammed his car off a steep embankment, killing him and a passenger instantly.

He had been the sole breadwinner, so when he died Annie was not only left without a husband and her children without a father, but also no income. Her job at the compound was an absolute lifesaver.

Once Mark had showed me around, he said, "Crocodile, I am sure you are dying to go to the beach."

I was. So I put on my bathing suit, covered by a sarong, and we headed off to the gate near the pool that led directly onto the shore. The gate was manned by security guards as the compound was under 24-hour surveillance, something common in many African countries. The beach was almost deserted with only a handful of people strolling past.

Mark and I sat down. With the building uncertainty about me leaving everything behind and nagging thoughts of 'What have I done?', I blurted out the main question on my mind.

"Tell me, what is so nice about Liberia? It is dirty and dilapidated, and very Third World."

37

Mark laughed, "You have only just got here! I know in a few days you will be happy."

I gave him the benefit of the doubt, despite my misgivings. At the moment I was just so happy to see him.

Mark then took me to a restaurant called The Golden Beach. It was right next door to the compound and a very popular venue for expats and locals to have sundowners, especially over the weekends.

He ordered drinks and the tropical setting lifted my mood. I looked around. Coconut trees, palm frond roofs, surf foaming on the golden beach in front of me, exotic cocktails being served from a beach bar – and right next door to where we lived.

What's there not to like?

Mark was right. This place certainly had potential.

Five

A FTER ONLY A FEW WEEKS, I was already settling in and loving being lazy in Liberia. Most of the time I spent unwinding.

I slept a lot, which showed exactly how exhausted I was from years of hard work and long hours running my own business. No doubt the change of climate from temperate Johannesburg to tropical Monrovia was quite an adjustment as well. Monrovia is only six degrees north of the equator.

I also did a lot of swimming in the giant-sized pool that was so luxuriously warm it felt like splashing in silk. When not swimming, I lazed in the sun. But instead of turning golden brown, thanks to my fair skin from an Irish/Scottish heritage, I got loads of freckles. Every day I had more to display.

Some days I would take a brisk walk along the beach. Mark demarcated a start and end point for my walks, not too far from the compound gate, which seemed safe enough.

The sea was beautiful, but unfortunately sometimes the tide brought in heaps of garbage that stretched halfway up the shore. As far as you could see, old shoes, toothbrushes,

39

hundreds of little plastic bags that the locals drank water from and broken glass which would slice though any bare feet, littered the golden beach.

But the dangers were not just pollution. One afternoon while Mark was fishing not far from the compound, I decided to go for a walk, keeping within the limits of the 'safe' area.

I had some cellphones and money in a carry bag which I covered with my towel and secured under my arm. Walking on the shoreline was an absolute joy, absorbing the beautiful view of the Atlantic and the warm sand squishing between my toes.

I turned as I reached the end of the area that Mark had demarcated, when I suddenly felt a powerful tug on my arm.

It was a man trying to grab my bag. With a surge of adrenalin, I spun around, kicking the culprit hard and giving a loud shriek.

I then kicked him again, aiming for his most vulnerable parts. He was not expecting that and quickly let go.

I started running towards Mark. Waving frantically to get his attention and my heart pounding like a piston, I felt as though I was running in surreal motion, like replays on a TV screen. No matter how hard I tried to pump my legs, I seemed to be hardly moving.

Mark glanced in my direction – and, thinking my wild waves were me just being friendly, waved back!

He only realized something was wrong when I collapsed on the sand. Dropping his fishing rod, he immediately sprinted over.

After giving me a couple of minutes to catch my breath, we walked back to the spot where I had been almost robbed. A Liberian woman who had seen the attack said that the man had run off down the beach and she doubted that we would catch him.

Mark agreed – the assailant-had without doubt by now run deep into the dunes.

After that Mark insisted that I no longer walk on the beach on my own. I couldn't really disagree as that had been a close call.

But we were able to see the lighter side of it all after I described where I had kicked the man.

He chuckled, "Don't mess with a South African girl."

Six

TWO MONTHS PASSED AND I was now well and truly in West African mode. We were meeting wonderful people.

The expats living in the compound soon became more than just friends. They were our extended family. They came from a whole host of different countries and we relied on each other for support, which was always given. There was a lot of laughter and loads of fun.

Late afternoons were spent trying out different menus for supper with the limited ingredients available in the country. That, coupled with my negligible cooking skills, meant spending some time preparing meals. I was no domestic goddess, like the TV celebrity chefs. Google became my recipe book and thankfully it was no concern for Mark to see that I had to Google how to cook an omelet.

There were a few exclusive supermarkets on the main road catering for expats and wealthy Liberians, where we shopped. These may have been well-stocked by Liberian standards, but certainly not what I was used to in Johannesburg. In fact, getting groceries and other necessities usually meant going to at least two of the supermarkets as none seemed to have everything under one roof. Certain items were also often sold out.

It was unlike any other shopping expedition I have ever experienced. And it certainly was an 'experience'. You got true VIP treatment with one person opening the door as you arrived, another packing your groceries, and someone else opening the door and bidding farewell as you left.

Despite the fertile land, 90 percent of food is imported, mainly due to lack of resources and the poor infrastructure. Farmers simply cannot get their produce to markets as the roads are so bad.

The staple diet of the country is rice, which is also mostly imported even though rice cultivation was once a thriving industry before the civil wars. Indeed, the different language labels on the array of goods on the shelves showed just how many countries Liberia imported its food from. Trying to understand packaging in French was challenging, but German was not too bad since I had learnt Afrikaans at school.

On my first few shopping trips, Peter was always right beside me to double-check that I was not getting short-changed. U.S. dollars as well as Liberian dollars were accepted, but the trickiest part in the beginning was learning to convert into a different currency and counting out the wads of Liberian notes which didn't buy very much. However, on a few occasions when I underestimated the cost of the groceries, it was not a problem. There was a lot of trust involved and the store owner would shrug and say I could bring the balance when I made my next shopping trip.

I also bought local fresh fruit and vegetables at a little store right next to one of the supermarkets. The choice was good; avocados, lemons, sweet potato, pumpkin, pineapples, potatoes, mangoes, monkey apples which look like red hairy lychees, and huge bananas half the size of my arm.

However, there are no malls anywhere in Liberia, so all non-grocery shopping had to be done in the town centers retail section.

Sadly, this was not much of a treat as Monrovia is not pretty. There is no glitter and glam. Wrecked shells of once beautiful office blocks, decrepit hotels and municipal buildings pockmarked with countless bullet holes are stark reminders of the remains of a once-thriving economy. Liberia was some time ago the most thriving country in West Africa. You would never have thought so today.

Besides the rundown, broken buildings, the town center – which is just called town – consists of many small shops and stalls with signs advertising wares scrawled onto the concrete walls of the buildings. Steel gates bolt the shops closed at night. Windows are tiny, if there are any.

Further down is an area known as Waterside, perhaps Liberia's most famous market. Nearby is a bridge over the Mesurado River, which flows through the capital, and driving over it provides a depressing backdrop of slums dwarfed by an Everest of litter on the edge of the river.

With 80 per cent of Liberians unemployed, a lot of people eke out a barely sustainable living from these micro businesses. Vendors hawk all kinds of stuff such as sunglasses, clothes and books, often displaying their goods on the dirt or grimy concrete sidewalks.

Fishmongers, mainly women, walk up and down the streets balancing large plastic bowls of fish on their heads, followed by squadrons of flies attracted by the pungent stench. The more entrepreneurial vendors use wheelbarrows to push their mini businesses around – bringing their wares to the customers, so to speak.

Liberia still has a vast contrast in living standards. There are a minority of very wealthy Liberians whose children are educated at foreign schools and universities, mostly in America and Canada. They shop at high end brand stores overseas and drive the latest model cars.

But for most, such affluence is from another planet. Their lives are a daily grind. An endless struggle of survival just to feed and bring up their families.

More often than not, families of five or more share a single-room shack or palm frond palaver huts, with no sanitation or running water. Many children don't go to school, consequently only half of all Liberians can read and write. Even those kids lucky enough to attend classes only get the most basic education and there are no extramural activities. Health care is also rudimentary and many youngsters die from curable diseases.

My first shopping trip to town wasn't what I expected. As soon as I got out of the car, I was bombarded by beggars. Expats are prime targets, and being blonde I stood out like a beacon. Even worse for me was that living with the constant threat of crime in Johannesburg, this sudden invasion of my space triggered instant alarm – as I believe it would for most South Africans.

Peter motioned for me to follow him and we hurriedly walked down the road into the store where I needed to shop.

Once that was done, I grabbed my bag and parcel and, clutching them as firmly as I could, we dashed back to the car.

Then while Peter was reversing out of the parking space, a beggar tried to force open my car door, his face squashed right up against the window. Fortunately, it was locked.

It was an 'interesting' baptism of fire, but after a few shopping trips I managed to relax as the beggars meant no harm. They were not violent or dangerous; they too needed to make a living. Despite the absolute poverty, crime in Liberia was nowhere near the appalling levels we have in South Africa.

However, after Mark heard about the beggar, he decided that I should have a bodyguard on future jaunts to the Waterside market.

We soon found one. He was called Pebbles, which was a big misnomer as he was more of a slab of granite than a small stone. Standing 1.96m tall and built like a Sherman tank, he was hulking enough to frighten anyone off.

Like so many Monrovians, Pebbles had been forced to fight in the bitter conflict on the side of the notorious warlord, Charles Taylor, who was President at the time. He told me that because of his imposing presence, he had the dreadful task of amputating Taylor's opponents' limbs, and one can only imagine the horror he had witnessed. (Charles Taylor is currently serving a 50-year jail term in Britain for crimes against humanity).

Despite Pebble's bulk and terrifying past, the person I got to know was a very kind soul with a gentle heart. A brave façade masked his troubled eyes.

I didn't know it at the time, but Pebbles would be a huge help to us in the traumatic times looming ahead – but in an entirely different role to the one he currently had as my trusty bodyguard.

Missy's farewell party and, below, Mark Missy and Mogli

Missy and I at the farm

Missy with Mogli and (below) learning to climb

At Golden Beach and (below) a bundle of cuteness

Seven

AS AN EXPAT, YOU CAN divorce yourself from any harsh truths you encounter and just say 'this is not my country'.

You can turn a blind eye to the poverty. You can turn away from the rampant disease and lack of education. You can ignore the cruelty to animals. You can say 'there's nothing I can do so I don't care what happens'.

Unfortunately for me, I soon discovered that I could not do that. Sometimes I wish I could, but like it or not, I had to come to terms with some unpalatable truths on the ground.

Which for me was the way animals were treated.

As much as I was aware that many wild animals were kept as caged pets in Liberia and bushmeat hunting and consumption was rife, nothing can prepare an animal lover like myself to see it first-hand.

Hunting is endemic in much of Liberia – almost a way of life – and bushmeat is considered a delicacy. It's easy to pass judgment, and I believe one should judge, but the sad fact is that in many poor countries, eating wild animals is a matter of survival.

However, the flipside of this reality is even more troubling. And that is most of the hunters are unaware that many animals they are slaughtering out of hand are top of the endangered species list. They have little concept that they are killing creatures that will soon go extinct if nothing is done to stop them.

Bushmeat is a very lucrative trade, despite the high health risk. Eating the flesh of many of the jungle animals can have potentially lethal consequences, such as catching AIDS, rabies, yellow fever and, of course, Ebola.

To give an idea of the scale of this slaughter, in Central and West Africa up to five million tons of bushmeat is consumed each year. Antelope, bats, monkeys, lemurs, crocodiles and other wild animals are killed by hunters in industrial numbers each day.

Before the First World gets too complacent about it only happening 'elsewhere', vast quantities of bushmeat are now also exported to other countries, including Europe and America, which is a potential backdoor entry for deadly Ebola

The first wild animal I saw that had been killed for bushmeat was while driving past a man trying to sell a slaughtered African civet on the side of the road. We were on the highway and I was appalled at the sight. I expressed my despair at the senseless slaying to Peter.

Peter gave me the Liberian explanation. "There be many starvin' peepl' who mus' feed dere fam'lies. Sellin' and eatin' bushmeat only way to surviv'."

Even though I knew that most Liberians hunted for survival, unlike so many westerners who hunt for trophies or sport, my anger got the better of me.

"Then they should stop having so many children," I snapped. "Why don't they raise chickens for eggs instead?"

Peter just looked at me.

"Huntin' is free."

On that occasion, I only saw the hunter from the comfort of my seat in our air conditioned car. The next time was far more vivid as I came face to face with a bushmeat seller.

I was at a pharmacy, although maybe calling it that was pushing it. It was little more than a tiny shop with a small stock of basic medicine.

As I was leaving, I saw a Liberian man holding two animals. To my horror they were still alive. The one was a pangolin, a critically endangered species and the most trafficked mammal in the world. These beautiful and inoffensive creatures are being hunted to the brink for food, traditional medicine and fashion accessories.

The other was an extremely rare Liberian mongoose.

Both animals were being held upside down by their tails, dangling from the hunter's hands. Both had a haunted, resigned look in their eyes. You could see that they knew their fate.

Watching the torturously uncomfortable manner that they were being handled set me off. I call it my 'Monster Moment'. It erupted with a vengeance.

"You are busy killing all of your animals," I shouted at the man. "How can you be so cruel? Look at how they are suffering!"

The hunter was, I would guess, a man in his 40s. His face was weathered from a hard life in the bush, his clothes stained with dirt and his pants shredded at the ankles.

He looked at me curiously at first, and then shrugged his shoulders. He showed absolutely no remorse. I don't think the emotion occurred to him. To him, this was just the way it was. If you kept the traumatized animals alive, their meat remained fresh for longer.

The absolute indifference he showed flamed my 'Monster Moment' further. I was shaking with rage. I felt so helpless that I started sobbing. With tears streaming down my face, I continued shouting at him.

"I am going to go to the authorities to tell them to arrest you. I wish you bad and I hope you go to Hell!"

This definitely got a response. The hunter was suddenly now also angry and began swearing at me. He then gestured with his head towards his machete that was leaning on the curb.

Blinded by rage, I had not noticed that before. This was no idle threat. At that instant I realized I could be in serious danger.

Peter hissed: "Ge' in de ca'!"

I obeyed. Then as Peter was leaving the parking space, I opened the window and flicked my hand at the hunter.

"I curse you!" I yelled.

Wow. That was a game changer. Peter's face widened in alarm. You simply do not curse a Liberian – particularly those who believe in witchcraft. I did not know if that included the hunter, but Peter was certainly not going to hang around to find out.

Mark had made it very clear to Peter that he was in charge of my safety whenever we were outside the compound. By cursing random bushmeat hunters, I was not exactly making it easy for him.

He sped off as fast as he could along Monrovia's chaotic roads.

The look on Peter's face said it all. I had put him in a potentially very difficult situation through no fault of his own.

I promised I would tell Mark that Peter had done all he could to diffuse the situation and he had really tried stop me from reacting to the bushmeat hunter's callous attitude.

But we both knew that wasn't going to stop the 'Monster Moment' erupting again.

I felt so helpless and frustrated knowing that there was nothing I could do to help these defenseless animals. When I asked Peter if he thought the hunter I had just cursed ever gave the two trussed-up animals any water, he shrugged his shoulders uncomfortably. He did not like such questions.

"Doan' tink so."

At least he was being honest with me.

I was still shaking from anger and despair, but realized that perhaps I had not handled the situation well. Witchcraft is said to be extensively practised by secret societies. In fact, every Liberian I asked said he or she believed it is still very much alive.

Although sorcery occurs throughout the country, it's most prevalent in Harper County, south of Monrovia and near the Cote D'Ivoire border. I was told that in some areas villagers live in constant fear of shadowy witchdoctors, especially as the main victims are children who are snatched from their homes in the middle of the night. The juvenile is then taken deep into the forest where he or she is ritualistically sacrificed by a witch or individual being initiated into the secret society.

The locals call this macabre slaying 'Gboyo'. The belief is that the power is in the blood and victims should be eaten alive. The heart is the most prized body part of all as it is said to give extra powers.

Gboyo is now fairly well documented as the warlord Charles Taylor's bloodthirsty militia had a gruesome reputation for eating human flesh to give them extra strength before going into battle. Despite global outrage and shock, it still continues.

So taking all that into account, the one thing you don't do in Liberia is publically curse someone, whether you believe in Gboyo or not.

On another occasion we passed two monkeys tied to a pole outside a house. They barely had enough rope to stand up straight, with no shelter or shade nearby. At that specific moment they were distracted from their awful predicament as they were eating fruit. Possibly a rare treat for them.

Even so, I wanted to talk to the residents of the house about this blatant cruelty and ask them to treat their animals with more compassion, but Peter wasn't having any of that and put his foot flat on the accelerator. Perhaps unsurprisingly, after the cursing incident Peter never again stopped in the streets if I saw animals in distress or being sold for bushmeat, no matter how much I urged.

He told me, as we sped off, that a lot of Liberians kept monkeys as well as chimps as pets and tying them up was normal. Most of these unfortunate animals spend their entire lives tethered to a rope or confined in a small cage.

By now it was clear to me that some Liberians believe that animals are only on Earth for people either to use or to eat. Or both.

This was not necessarily innate cruelty or maliciousness on their part. It was genuine ignorance. And that, as well as the fact that their own children were hungry, made it extremely difficult – if not impossible – to change their minds about animal welfare in the short term.

Even so, I took every chance I could to try and persuade them to treat our fellow travelers on this planet with more compassion.

It's not only bushmeat slaughter that is driving Liberia's wildlife to extinction. There's also a thriving industry in selling forest creatures for pets. As well, of course, as a growing illegal logging industry destroying their habitat.

Take the case of Fadi Chdid, a good friend who lived in an apartment opposite to ours, who had bought an African Grey parrot from a hunter. He had done so out of extreme concern for the abused bird that probably would have died if he had not intervened.

That, sadly, is the Catch 22 scenario. Many well-intentioned expats who come across an animal that has been caught by a hunter, and usually in terrible condition, buy the creature in order to save it. If they don't the animal or bird will perish.

The problem is that once a Good Samaritan parts with money, the hunter returns to the forest to catch another animal, or more likely many others, to sell to other compassionate people.

Like most of the poor creatures caught and taken out of the wild, Fadi's parrot was totally traumatized. He managed to find it a cage, but it was too small and the miserable parrot spent its first few days at the compound barely able to move. It could not fly as its wings had been brutally clipped by the hunter, so setting it free was not an option.

Fadi named the parrot Charlie, and despite his best efforts, the unfortunate bird was understandably extremely distressed. When Fadi left for work each day he put Charlie's cage outside under shade. I could hear it squawking pitifully from our apartment.

To make matters worse, Charlie could hear the indigenous parakeets that were often high up in the trees at the compound, which obviously agitated him even more. He was a prisoner in a tiny cage trying to escape, but couldn't fly off. Trying to console him was hopeless.

Fortunately, Fadi managed to find a bigger cage and after a few weeks Charlie settled down a little.

Then Fadi had a stroke of luck. A good friend – to both him and us and also called Fadi, although fortunately with a different surname, Hassan, was going back home to Lebanon. The two Fadis decided it would be better for Charlie to go with him and live with Fadi Hassan's father who had cared for birds before. They organized the necessary permits and even though Charlie isn't free, he settled down quickly in Lebanon.

According to Fadi's father, backed up by a video clip, Charlie is thankfully now a happy, well-loved parrot. So it wasn't the ideal ending, but at least it was a happy one. Something unusual for much of Liberia's wild life.

One thing is certain; West Africa's unique fauna is in grave danger. To save creatures one at a time, such as what Fadi did with Charlie, is at least doing something.

The only long term solution is to change the mindset of people. To somehow get them to understand that animals are not on Earth only to be killed or kept as traumatized pets. I wanted to get involved in doing that.

Unknown to me, that was soon going to happen. With a vengeance.

Eight

I GOT AN IDEA OF HOW difficult it would be to control the rampant bushmeat hunting when I accompanied Mark on a short business trip to the interior during May.

Mark needed to check on some of the smaller outlets of the company he worked for and he had to do so before the rainy season started. Liberia has some of the flimsiest infrastructure in the world and when the rains come from the end of May to mid-November, many roads are impassable, even with 4x4s.

An hour or so out of Monrovia, we were deep into the rainforest. As far as you could see an endless panorama of thick, verdant jungle flanked both sides of the road with towering magnificence. It looked impenetrable, although every now and again the dense forest landscape would be split by elephant grass, or swamps studded with awesome gnarly-rooted mangrove trees.

You would think the same view, mile after mile, would become boring, but it wasn't. I have seldom been so entranced and engrossed. I was in a truly wild African rainforest. It was euphoric. This was real 'Gorillas in the Mist' country, just not as mountainous. But it was easily as impressive as anything you would have seen in the Dian Fossey movie. In fact, even more so because this was the real deal.

Sadly, so too was the real deal wildlife tragedy lurking behind the thick green foliage. I could imagine the forest hunters out there, shooting or catching rapidly disappearing creatures like the pangolin or mongoose that-I had seen on the sidewalks of Monrovia.

The Earth looked so vibrant, so full of life. But it was a façade. The death and slaughter behind the lush curtain was happening on an industrial scale. Even though the jungle was still there, impervious and imposing as ever, its once bountiful wildlife was going. Going fast.

About seven hours into the journey, we arrived at two reed huts where locals were selling a variety of fruit. It was the equivalent of a jungle shopping center.

Peter stopped so we could buy something to eat.

We got out of the car and I noticed a wide-eyed young boy staring at me. Peter said something to him and then laughed at the reply. He told me that the little boy was amazed that there were people with 'hair like the sun'. He had never seen a blonde before. To him, I was an apparition.

I smiled at him. Then the irony hit me. He had never seen a blonde woman before – but one day his descendants may stare with the same awe at a jungle animal. Perhaps even this child may never see a pangolin again, if he ever had. It will soon be a lot rarer in his life than a blonde woman.

Standing there outside a reed hut in the rainforest eating a mango, I started to think dark thoughts: would the bushmeat trade ever be stopped before all the jungle creatures were killed? How would it be policed, even if there was the political will to do so?

Where would you even start?

There was no proper infrastructure to speak of. For at least the past six hours Peter had been threading his way through bumpy, dirt tracks riddled with potholes the size of craters, some stretching across the entire width of the road.

Indeed, sometimes the only way to get through the quagmires was to drive with two wheels off the verge. At times we were titling at 30 degree angles.

So imagine trying to get game rangers and policemen into the area to do regular anti-poaching patrols and prosecuting perpetrators.

Several hours later we arrived in Ganta, close to the Guinea border and the second largest city in Liberia.

That evening we went to eat at a recommended restaurant. I'm not sure who recommended it, but it looked more like a canteen than anything else

It was already dark, and the only lights were single naked bulbs hanging by a cable on some small reed huts. Locals used their cell phone flashlights if they wanted to see where they were going.

The menu did not spoil you for choice. There were three dishes; goat's head soup, fish, and chicken, with a side dish option of chips or rice.

In fact, it turned out that the menu was misleading. There were, in fact, only two selections as the chicken was finished. That left us with suspect soup or fish.

I didn't have to consider the alternatives for long. Goat's head soup would never be on my bucket gourmet list, even if I was suffering from malnutrition. So fish it was.

Our meal arrived. If I had to guess the species, I would have gone for piranha. The entire fish – head, eyes and gaping mouth displaying teeth – was served whole on the plate.

I soon found out why. All the other diners, including children, ate absolutely everything. Even the bones.

The next day we drove back to civilization in Monrovia.

Then the rainy season started in deadly earnest. Most mornings began with misty skies or pelting tropical downpours, which didn't leave much to do except wait inside for better days.

Monrovia is one of the wettest capitals in the world. The rainfall in June alone can be double the rainfall of London – which is not exactly known for its glorious sunshine.

Every day seemed the same. Wet or even wetter, with endless, bucketing rain creating millions of miniature lakes wherever there were gaps or crevices in the ground.

Roads throughout the city were now little more than swirling, muddy tracks or gushing rivulets of litter with more junk eddying down the freeways like toxic rafts than vehicles.

Mark managed to get me an oversized pair of gumboots to wade through the water. It was my most essential item of footwear.

All we could do was sit back and hope that the sunshine would one day return.

It did. In November. It's one of the most glorious sights imaginable after months of bleak gray skies.

I suddenly realized that I had now been in the country for eight months. It had done me a world of good. It's amazing what recharging your personal batteries and minimal stress – apart from seeing abused animals hawked on roadsides – can do to you, both physically and mentally.

I felt on top of the world.

Nine

W E WERE HAVING SUCH fun that Mark suggested his two youngest children come out for a visit during the December school holidays.

His daughter Sydney Rose was now 10 and his son David eight. It would be a great adventure for them.

We chatted to Anne, the children's mother, assuring her that they would be safe. She gave her consent and the decision was made; David and Sydney were coming to Liberia.

They arrived early the next month, extremely excited about their exotic holiday. We were equally excited to see them. They soon fell in love with Liberia. Not only was it fantastic to be with their dad again, but it was tremendous fun living in an apartment just a stone's throw from the beach as well a huge swimming pool to jump into whenever they wished. And right on their doorstep.

Mark had made a list of places that he thought the kids would enjoy. Top choice was a beautiful farm, where we already were spending a lot of our spare time. We had first discovered it some months ago and made friends with the owners, Jack and Dorothy.

We became even more involved when Jack discovered that Mark was a scratch golfer and asked if he would help in project-managing a course that he was building on the farm.

Mark jumped at the chance. Few fanatical golfers get the opportunity to build their dream course, and so for Mark this was the scenario of the proverbial kid in a candy store, multiplied by a million.

Mark was there most weekends overseeing his pet project. The fairways, greens and driving range were taking shape, while construction of the clubhouse was also coming along nicely.

Then Jack, a very wealthy man with various businesses, asked Mark to leave his job with the company that had brought him to Liberia and work for him. He said he believed that Mark would be a great asset to his business.

Mark considered the offer, and even though I liked Jack, my instincts told me something wasn't right. However, Mark was more trusting and believed it would be a good career move and it was triple his current salary.

He took the job.

Jack's farm was more like a tourist attraction than an actual working ranch, with lots of fun activities and thus ideal for Sydney and David.

From my side, I was relatively relieved to see that for the most part the farm animals were fairly well cared for, although the horses looked a bit thin. My heart went out to them having to take people for long rides along the grassland in the extreme heat.

Besides the usual farm animals, there were four small separate enclosures housing two crocodiles and a caiman, and another where Jack kept a python. On one visit I peered in and watched the massive snake for some time. I had never seen a python so close up and was awed by its impressive size and imposing presence, even though it never seemed to move.

That Saturday – in fact, almost every Saturday – a Kiddies Camp was held providing a whole host of outdoor activities for children. David and Sydney were looking forward to it, but their enthusiasm was dampened when we arrived and saw a baboon tied to a tree near the gate.

I had seen the baboon before and had actually voiced my concerns to Dorothy about it. I firmly believe that animal lovers have to speak up for those creatures whom cannot speak. If we don't, who will?

However, I didn't achieve much as Dorothy somewhat abruptly brushed my unease aside saying that it was her husband's problem. She had enough already on her plate.

One consolation was that the baboon was tethered to a big shady tree with a long enough piece of rope to give it some freedom of movement.

Seeing the forlorn creature just sitting there with a rope around its neck really upset David and Sydney. Despite the sad situation, I was delighted to see that both kids cared so much about animals.

Sydney and I then went to the stables where children were having horse riding lessons. Bursting with excitement, she was lifted into the saddle and a groom led her for a few laps around the arena and then down a long sandy road and back. I was pleased to see that the horses were not being overworked, particularly on such a hot day.

When Sydney returned, the huge smile said it all. After dismounting, she said she "reeeaaaally" wanted to come back for another ride.

David and Mark later joined us at the swimming pool just as Sydney and I were dipping in. We had a bite to eat, then it was time to leave.

Driving past a little bridge towards the exit, something caught my eye. Something I will never forget. Something that changed our lives irrevocably.

"Peter stop the car!"

Peter slammed on brakes. Then I saw clearly what had just caught my attention. It was a woman holding a baby chimpanzee.

Mark buried his head in his hands. He knew exactly where this was going, and that it would probably end in tears.

Peter had the same look on his face as he had when I confronted the bushmeat hunter with the pangolin and mongoose downtown. I could see him thinking, "Oh dear, the crazy monster is about to emerge again." If he could have, I reckon he would have accelerated off.

I got out of the car to look closer. The bundle of cuteness, only a few months old, peered back at me. It was love at first sight,

I asked the woman, "Where did you get the chimp from?"

Her reply ripped my heart. She said Jack had bought her from a hunter when he saw that she appeared to be sick. Originally there had been two orphaned babies, and I tried not to think what had happened to the other one. I didn't want to know, as I suspected the worst.

Jack then assigned the baby animal to the woman to take care of. I asked if I could hold the tiny creature.

She let me take her. As the little chimpanzee clung to my side, I gazed down into her trusting eyes. I was mesmerized by the look she gave me.

Soon I was sobbing – sobbing for the loss of her family while raging against the hunter and cruel, heartless people who had put this helpless orphan in such an awful situation.

I sobbed for the fact that for the rest of her life this small, innocent creature would be reliant on humans, the murderers of her kind.

I sobbed for the destruction of so many other jungle animals that are being hunted mercilessly to extinction.

I sobbed because I felt so helpless about it all; that the trusting look on her face as I held her was misplaced. I was a human – the species responsible for her miserable plight.

Suddenly, my carefree life in Liberia came shuddering to a halt. I knew at the instant I had to do something.

I had to make sure this innocent orphan would be okay, otherwise I simply would not be able to live with myself. I could no longer be a bystander.

"Does she have a name?" I asked the woman.

She replied, "Her name is Missy,"

Ten

S TILL SOBBING, I THEN ASKED the woman, who looked a little bemused by my reaction, "What is your name?"

"Adele."

Adele told me that Missy had now been in her care for two weeks. The baby was not that well at the moment and had been coughing badly. Fortuitously, a vet happened to be on the farm that day doing routine checks on the health of Jack's other animals. He had examined Missy and said it was just a respiratory infection and not too serious.

Despite the heat, Missy was wearing a baby's vest.

"Why is she wearing a vest?" I asked

"Missy ha' ches' 'fection. Ves' keep her warm."

It was sweltering, but I didn't question the caring gesture. Instead I politely mentioned that it probably wasn't necessary in the hot weather.

The tiny bundle was nibbling on a biscuit and I watched in amazement how human-like her actions were.

"What does Missy eat?" I asked.

The answer stung. "Missy normal' eat banan', biskit an' milk. But milk an' de banan' finish'."

Adele then said she hoped to get money from the farm manager for more food the following day.

Without hesitation, Mark dug into his pocket and gave her a fistful of Liberian dollars, making it very clear that the money was for milk.

To get her out of the blistering heat, I took Missy to sit in the air-conditioned car with me for a few minutes.

Then it was time to go and reluctantly I handed the beautiful furry bundle back to Adele, who no doubt was feeling the effects of the extreme heat herself. She was not young. I would guess she was close to 70. Although she was called a security guard, she was probably more of a gate opener. Being an elderly woman, she would hardly be able physically to defend right of entry.

As we left, I told her I would return on Monday with milk and bananas.

On our way back to the Ocean View compound, David and Sydney didn't complain once about the long, spine-jarring trip. Instead, unsure of how to react to my tears, they sweetly tried to console me.

All Mark said was, "Crocodile, this is going to end in heartache!"

I said nothing. Deep down, I had a horrible feeling that he might be right.

But there was nothing I could do to stop my inner emotional turmoil. It was an irrational rollercoaster ride, and I felt as though I was being drawn inexorably into a situation I had no control of.

Back at the compound I tried to stop fretting that Missy wouldn't get enough milk over the weekend. I knew I was being stupid as it was only two days. I would see her again when I went back to the farm on Monday.

But until then, David and Sydney Rose deserved a fun holiday. I was determined not to ruin that by being a stick-in-the-mud.

Eleven

TO GET MY MIND OFF MISSY, we arranged to take Sydney and David to the Libassa Ecolodge the next day.

It is highly recommended by all expats, although it's only open in summer as muddy roads make it inaccessible during the rainy season.

The lodge is a jewel and shows what Liberia could be like in a better world. It's a snapshot of the country's true beauty. As the gate opens, a glimpse of paradise awaits you. The entrance is a walkway of beach sand, lined with thickets of palms and trees leading to a little bridge over a running stream. Then you reach the lodge which is built entirely from wood.

The cabins, where guests stay, rest on thick stilts with palm frond roofs surrounded by the virgin forest. You feel as if you are an integral part of the natural world.

A trail leads from the lodge to a lagoon so large that at times all you can see is a glittering expanse of mirror-smooth water. A wooden deck with loungers and a minibar is there to help appreciate the stunning view even more.

The owners of the lodge, Rudolph Antoune and Lisa Viau Antoune are wonderful, caring people who have a big heart for animals. It shows in everything they do in their piece of Eden.

The lodge had also recently acquired an inflatable canoe and swimming and rowing in a pristine Atlantic lagoon was an experience I hoped Sydney and David would treasure forever.

Despite their initial fear of snakes and crocodiles lurking in the tranquil waters, they soon were happily splashing around. The day was crammed with endless fun.

Rudolph and Lisa had recently started building enclosures for smaller animals confiscated from hunters or abusive owners and which were in dire need of rehabilitation. Rudolph then took us for a walk to show the new project and even though there were currently only two enclosures under construction, it was something Liberia desperately required. At last, a sanctuary was being established to care for small wild animals that would have otherwise died. There was nothing else like it in the country.

There's no doubt about it: the Ecolodge was my favorite place in Liberia. On that glorious sunny day, I think everyone agreed with me.

The next morning, I woke up excited that I was going to see Missy.

Peter came to fetch me and Mark couldn't resist wryly commenting on how 'suddenly' the back-breaking drive on dirt roads to the farm didn't seem 'so bad' anymore.

I just smiled, but it was true. On several previous occasions I had chosen not to go to the farm with Mark because of the uncomfortable and sometimes scary trip. Now I couldn't wait to get there.

Annie stayed at our apartment to look after David and Sydney while Peter drove me to the supermarket to get more baby milk formula, a teat bottle, and fruit.

Then we were off to see Missy.

When we arrived she was clinging to Adele's side at the security hut next to the gate. I was relieved that she looked a lot better and her chest infection seemed to have cleared.

Equally pleasing was to see that Adele had bought milk formula with the money Mark had given her. Missy was drinking it from a cup.

I gave Adele the extra milk and teat-bottle. To my delight I got an "oo oo" from Missy, which I soon discovered was her way of saying 'hello'.

We then sat on the grass. Missy looked content with Adele, sitting on her lap and playing with her dress puller.

This was also heartwarming as it showed that Adele genuinely cared for her little charge.

However, there were other concerns. For example, Adele told me she had spoken to the farm manager about Missy's milk running out and he said he had not received money from Jack.

I tried to calm my anger. What would have happened if we had not driven past when we did on Saturday? If Mark had not given Adele money, Missy would have had no proper meal for the entire weekend. She also had an infection at the time – would that have got even worse if she'd had no milk, her staple diet?

I couldn't help once again thinking that maybe fate had drawn us together.

I asked to hold her and she willingly came to me. She was the cutest creature I had ever seen; her perfect ears, wide soulful eyes … the freckles on her face. She was gorgeous.

However, we could not stay for too long as I could see Missy was tired. She was just a baby and Adele confirmed that she would now be needing a nap.

As I left, I told Adele that she must call me if she wanted anything for Missy, and that we would be returning to the farm in five days' time.

Friday finally arrived – not quick enough for me – and Sydney and I both woke up extremely excited. For different reasons, though. Sydney was looking forward to another horse ride, while I just wanted to see Missy.

Not taking any chances, I phoned Adele to make sure that Missy would be at the farm. Adele said yes, and once again asked me to bring more milk and fruit. It seemed the farm manager still had not given her money for Missy's food. This set off alarm bells jangling in my head. Missy was, at the very least, pretty low down in the pecking order of the farm's commitments.

After a quick dash into the supermarket, we were on our way.

Despite the bumpy drive, I started getting more and more animated as we got closer to the farm. Peter dropped me off at the security building while Mark, Sydney and David went to the restaurant to meet Dorothy.

To my delight, Missy recognized me from the last meeting and gave me another "oo oo" chimp greeting.

Adele then introduced me to her son Jonathan, who also worked at the farm. She said she was not well and needed to go to the clinic, so Jonathan would be looking after Missy in her absence.

Knowing that Missy's immature immune system was not strong and that chimpanzees can catch some of our germs, I suggested that I take her home with me, instead of that chore falling on Jonathan.

Adele seemed pleased with the idea, but said she needed to confirm if it was okay with Jack.

I phoned Peter to fetch me at the gate. With Adele's permission, I took Missy with me to meet Mark and the kids at the restaurant.

I sat down next to Mark with Missy clutching my side. He leaned over and said exactly what I was thinking: how bittersweet it was to have the privilege of holding a baby chimp, but at the same time knowing that she belonged in the wild with her family.

I nodded. It was the mirror of my thoughts

I passed her over to him and he couldn't stifle his delighted grin when holding her. He even tried to speak to her in his version of chimp talk – 'chimpanese' – to get another hello.

To my astonishment, it worked. Missy responded with an "oo oo".

While he was playing with Missy, I whispered to him my intention to take her home as Adele was not well. Missy was at serious risk of catching Adele's germs.

Mark nodded, still having a 'chimp chat' with Missy.

Then without hesitation, he asked Dorothy, who luckily was also at the restaurant, if I could take care of Missy while Adele was off sick. Dorothy said she had no problem with that, but Jack would have to agree.

That was promising. Both Dorothy and Adele had agreed, so surely Jack would also say yes.

Mark said he would phone Jack as soon as we got to the security office so Adele could hear directly from her boss what the answer was.

Dorothy then told me that one of her daughter's had wanted to keep Missy in their home as a pet, but her children and dogs were already enough of a handful without a baby chimp adding to the burden. That explained why Adele had been given the job, and why Missy was kept at the security office. The word 'burden' also said loads to me about what they actually thought of Missy.

It was finally time to go. We stopped at the gate to drop Missy off with Adele while Mark phoned Jack.

They spoke for a while and then Mark turned to me, "Jack says it's fine. You can take Missy home."

Just like that! I couldn't believe it.

Mark then passed the phone to Adele so that she too could hear Jack's instructions.

At last I had the privilege of spending some decent time with Missy.

Sitting in the car on the way home, I stared into her eyes, wondering what her thoughts were. She already seemed very content on my lap. In fact, she hadn't complained at all when we left Adele, who at that stage was her surrogate mother.

Peter stopped at the supermarket for me to buy a pile of diapers. I have no children of my own and never thought that I would see the day when I would have to buy a bulk-load of nappies. But at the same time, I hated the fact that I had to subject Missy, a wild animal, to wearing them.

As soon as we got home, I went straight to the air conditioner to turn down the temperature. I wasn't taking any chances with her getting sick, especially as she had just recovered from a cold and had been in close contact with Adele, who by her own admission was not well.

Later that afternoon we took a walk to the swimming pool and Missy was soon the center of attraction. Many of the expats were thrilled to see her, saying how unbelievably cute she was.

Sadly, that is exactly what the unscrupulous hunters in the rainforests bank on. It's a trap many expats and urban Liberians fall for; our natural compassion for an orphaned animal makes us want to help it. Sadly, most do not know that once the hunter has sold one baby creature, he's off into the bush to catch another.

Missy was in big demand for photographs and 'selfies', but I was reluctant to hand her over because of germs that her vulnerable immune system may not cope with. I continuously washed her hands with disinfectant and brought along an antibacterial spray for anyone who might touch her.

Also – and just as importantly – I didn't want to give the impression that she was my pet. Or that a chimp should ever be a pet.

That evening Mark made a cot from a large plastic container. He fluffed it with pillows and a throw but Missy was having none of that. She wanted to be in bed with us.

It was understandable. Like all baby chimps, she needed to cling and cuddle, as she would have done with her mother and family in the forests. In her mind, her place was right there alongside us, her new family.

So we let her into our bed and she hung onto me for the entire night. I spent most of the time awake, just lying still and watching her, besides giving her milk when she woke and changing her diaper.

She was up early in the morning, content and playful. Despite the little sleep I'd had, the pleasure of spending time with her really energized me. I felt totally alive, as if I'd had the most peaceful night in the world.

Missy gulped down her bottle of milk, followed by some fruit.

The cot was then turned into a playpen, as it was pretty obvious Missy had no intention of sleeping in it while our bed was nearby.

She loved it. She would climb over the top and then deliberately topple over with the chimp equivalent of a big grin, then get up off the makeshift mattress and climb out, then do it all over again.

She also had endless fun playing with a towel, covering her head and then finding her way out again. When she emerged, or if the towel fell off, she would give us a cute cheeky look and then cover herself again.

Another of her favorite gigs was playing with a belt. She would hold onto the top end and when I lifted the belt, she would scramble down using her arms just as a chimp would do on a branch in the jungle.

She was as delightful as a mischievous toddler. She had taken my heart.

I was not sure if I would ever get it back.

Twelve

L UKE, ONE OF THE OWNERS OF OCEAN View, invited us to his home for lunch the next day.

He had two compounds that he co-owned with his business partner, John. During the week he stayed at Ocean View, while most weekends he went to the other compound on the far side of town, which was where we were going to meet him and his wife Helena.

But now, somewhat unexpectedly, we had an extra guest. So Mark phoned Luke to ask if we could bring a baby chimp along. Completely unfazed, he said of course we could.

I felt as if I had become a mother overnight. This was the first time we were going anywhere with Missy and it was like setting off on a major expedition. I packed a bag with her milk, snacks, extra diapers and a towel, then washed her hands with antibacterial soap. In the past, Mark and I would simply jump into the car and drive off.

Luke and Helena were wonderful hosts. They loved having people over, taking great delight in serving up trays of traditional Lebanese cuisine that were absolutely mouthwatering.

Luke was in his early 70s and Helena about 20 years younger. A very attractive woman who had clearly taken care of herself, she always looked like a million dollars and as if she had just been to the hairdresser.

Lunch was a feast and scooping up the array of different dishes with Lebanese bread was a glorious assault on the tastebuds.

Both our hosts were absolutely fascinated with Missy, amazed at her uncanny resemblance to a human baby. This is one of the most visceral reactions people have to chimpanzees – how alike they are to us. They are considered the closest relative to humans, which, to me, makes the human race's appalling treatment of them even more bizarre.

After lunch Mark, Luke, Sydney and David went out onto the lagoon in Luke's speedboat, while I stayed behind with Missy and Helena.

While Missy had her afternoon nap on my lap, Sydney and David had the time of the lives on the boat, marveling at how far the lagoon stretched and how fast the speedboat could go. David was given a turn to drive, which made his day. He was now a 'skipper'.

Later, back in our apartment, I phoned Adele to see how she was. She said that she was better and asked if I could bring Missy back on Tuesday.

My heart sank. I know I should have been happy that Adele was recovering, but I was devastated that I had to give Missy back.

In such a short time, I had already become completely devoted to her. Mark reminded me of his remark when I first saw Missy; that this could end in bitter tears.

I didn't want to think about it.

The staff at the compound, and for that matter most Liberians, called Missy a 'buboon'. I had to correct them on numerous occasions, explaining that she was actually a chimpanzee, which is very different to a baboon.

Although a few of the staff were afraid of her, most really enjoyed having Missy around. It wasn't always a positive experience, however, as there was a security guard who boasted to me that he had a contact who could get us baby chimps for pets anytime we wanted. I angrily retorted that a chimp should never under any circumstance be a pet. Mark's constant plea that I try and calm down before lashing out at such ignorance stopped me from losing it altogether with the man, although at first I did feel like ripping his head off.

However, I did tell the security guard that with the relentless slaughtering of the beautiful creatures in his country, it would not be long before people such as his 'contact' will have killed off all the animals in the forests. Or sold their progeny to be roped up in the cities for the rest of their miserable lives.

Tuesday arrived and it was time to take Missy back to the farm. I woke with dread, Missy latched tightly onto me. Her facial expressions told me so much. She definitely loved being with us as much as we loved having her.

That made giving her back even more difficult. How was I going to cope with her away on the farm coupled the constant worry that she was not being looked after or fed properly?

For my own peace of mind, I now really needed to know what Jack planned to do in the long term. The uncertainty was tearing me apart.

However, I wasn't sure whether Jack himself knew what he was going to do with Missy when she grew up. Tie her up like his staff had done with the baboon?

Adele looked better and was obviously happy to have Missy back. There definitely was a bond between them, which was great to see, especially as in several days' time we were going home for two weeks, taking Mark's kids back with us. I had to know that Missy would be okay when I was away.

I handed Missy over to Adele, saying goodbye with as much composure as I could muster, despite my anguish. I promised to visit on Friday with more milk before we left for South Africa.

The next day I woke, cramped up with a stomach bug. Doubled over and feeling dreadful, I somehow managed to drag myself out of bed. I was determined to make sure Sydney and David enjoyed the last few days of their holiday.

We were initially scheduled to fly back home for two weeks, which I was dreading as it seemed a long time to be away from Missy. But I had a plan. I said to Mark that as most of our family and friends were going elsewhere on holiday over Christmas, there would not be that many people to visit. So I suggested we should shorten our trip.

Mark is no fool, knowing full well that the real reason I wanted to do this was because I was reluctant to be away from Missy for long.

Luckily for me, he was also reasonably flexible. Liberia had us hooked. Mark's analogy that the country has superglue in the sand was very apt.

In fact, if the truth be known, the compound more than South Africa was our new home. A home that happened to be right on the beach with wonderful neighbors and beautiful, hot sunny days for much of the year.

So he agreed. We would only go back for a week. We changed our return ticket for the day after Christmas, and with a stayover in Ghana, we would be back in Liberia on December 28.

Just before leaving, we made another trip to the farm. Missy was with Jonathan, who seemed competent and told us how he loved to play with her. He assured me that Missy would be fine with him and I had no need whatsoever to worry about being so far away.

Sydney and David's last day in Liberia was December 22. Our flight was at night, with a short stopover in Ghana and we would then catch a connecting flight to Johannesburg from Kenya. I sat next to Sydney on the window seat, while David and Mark sat in the middle aisle.

Sydney was very subdued and when the air hostess came around with the dinner trolley, she refused food. She said she had a headache and wasn't feeling well. I also didn't want anything to eat as I still had a slight tummy problem. But now I was really worried that Sydney had caught my bug.

David obviously had no such problems. He ordered the pepper chicken. Unbeknown to him, West African pepper is pretty fiery. His first mouthful left him spluttering, but that did not deter him. Soon sweat was streaming down his forehead. His eyes widened with each sizzling chew, but somehow he finished the entire meal. Mark and I watched with awe. And amusement.

When we landed in Ghana the captain announced our take-off schedule for Kenya had been delayed. What should have been a 30-minute wait turned into an impatient hour-and-a-half.

Sydney looked a little pale and when I put a hand on her forehead, it felt a bit warm. Fortunately, I had brought along some medicine which I gave to her. Soon after takeoff she fell asleep.

I woke her up just before we landed at the Jomo Kenyatta International airport in Nairobi. To my alarm, she was now burning up with a fever.

When then discovered that we had missed our connecting flight due to the earlier delay in Ghana. This was serious stuff with a sick child, especially as we had no idea what was wrong with her. It was an extremely anxious three-hour wait in the transit lounge for the next flight out.

Luckily I always travel with a jacket, which I wrapped around Sydney who was now shivering uncontrollably with alternating hot and cold flushes.

When we finally arrived in Johannesburg she was still burning up, and I was worried sick that she had caught malaria or some other serious tropical disease while in our care.

Her mother was at the airport and I was very happy to hand her over.

Once home, she was diagnosed with Strep Throat, and to our infinite relief, she recovered quickly.

Thirteen

CHRISTMAS WAS SOON OVER, AND it was a good decision to shorten our trip with most of our friends and family being away.

Arriving back at the compound was a pleasure. In such a short space of time, Liberia now felt like home.

I phoned Adele to see how Missy was. To my alarm, she said she didn't know as she was in town looking after her sister who was ill. As a result, Jonathan was taking care of Missy.

I immediately phoned Jonathan who assured me that Missy was fine. However, he said he was going to a funeral over the weekend, but a friend of his would take care of Missy while he was away.

I was not happy about that. I said I would fetch Missy first thing in the morning. Jonathan agreed that would be a good idea, and then told me that Missy had run out of milk.

I bit my tongue and said nothing. I knew for a fact that I had left more than enough money for milk while we were away. I would find out what the problem was in the morning.

Peter dropped Mark off at the office, and after a quick stop at the supermarket to buy milk, we were on our way. I wished the trip to the farm wasn't so far as I was always impatient to get to Missy.

I was shocked when I saw her. In just a few days she had lost weight and her eyes were dull. She grabbed the milk I gave her and gulped it down, obviously extremely hungry. The happy, contented Missy I had handed over to Adele a week ago was now weak and forlorn.

If that wasn't bad enough, she also had a cut on her lip and a wound on her back. Jonathan told me that she had been kicked by a donkey.

"How did a donkey kick her?" I asked, exasperated.

"She be playin' on de grass and de donkey cam close. She then got frigh' and de donkey kick her," was his reply.

It did not sound the likeliest of stories. Forget about Mark telling me to have 'composure', my blood boiled and I told Jonathon straight out how irresponsible it was to have left Missy unattended.

Missy clung to me feebly as we got into the car. I gave her a banana on the way home, which she ate with some enthusiasm and I was relieved that at least she still had an appetite. I then covered her with a towel and she snuggled contently in my arms.

Nearing the main road, she seemed to regain some of her former vitality, looking around to investigate what was happening around her as she always did. She then gazed into my eyes with an intensity that bored deep into me. My heart lurched.

I returned the look and mouthed a vow that I would do whatever I could to protect her and make sure that she had a loving, caring environment for the rest of her life.

Before returning to the compound, we popped into Mark's office so he could see her. She happily went to him, much to his delight. He had missed her as well.

Missy slept for the rest of the day. Annie also noticed how she had deteriorated so quickly, sharing my anger at how irresponsibly she had been taken care of.

"It no' right," she said. "They no good fo' her."

My main focus now was to get Missy's strength back. Mark and I carefully examined the sore on her back and both agreed it looked like a bite, not a kick as Jonathan had said.

But it was difficult to tell how she received the cut on her lip. Fortunately, I had some antiseptic cream to rub on the wound, and it soon started healing nicely.

By Sunday morning she was already looking much stronger and her eyes had regained their spark. But her rapid deterioration in the week we had been away really spooked me. No longer did I allow her to be passed over to anyone other than Annie and Mark. Being so irresistible, I knew how much people wanted to touch and hold her, and not wanting to take any chances, I regularly washed her hands with disinfectant.

I also asked anyone coming close to her if they had a cold or flu, as chimpanzees can catch our germs and vice versa. However, chimps don't have the same resistance as we do and what is a run-of-the-mill ailment for us can be fatal for them.

That evening Mark asked again how I was going to cope with having to take Missy back to the farm.

I shook my head, "She can't go back. She will die!"

He nodded in agreement. It was pretty obvious she was not being looked after properly. Even though Missy 'belonged' to Jack, I knew that somehow I had to persuade him to release her into my care

Mark suggested I phone Jack and just ask him straight out if I could take her. It was the right thing to do, so the next day I went to the office with Mark to speak directly to Jack about Missy's future.

I was very nervous, but Mark was optimistic.

"He always has time for you, Crocodile. He always has a big smile when he sees you."

I hoped today would be no exception.

Jack is a very busy man, but on that day luck was on my side. As we arrived at the office, he fortuitously happened to be in his car at the parking lot, right in front of the entrance where I was standing with Missy.

He gave me a smile and I knew this was my big chance. It was now or never. I tried not to fumble and blabber too much, a habit I have when I am anxious. With a shaky voice I plucked up my courage.

"Jack, would there be any chance I could take care of Missy? She has not been taken care of properly. I can take good care of her."

Jack barely hesitated. He gave me another smile and said, "You have carte blanche. I know you will look after her well."

Simple as that. Missy was now, at last, completely in my care.

"Thank you from the bottom of my heart," was all I could think of to say. Yet I knew that was all that needed to be said.

I almost had to pinch myself. Being given carte blanche was more than I dared to hope would ever happen.

I could get her a future that she deserved. I could now do the one thing I wanted more than anything else.

I could return her to her own kind.

Fourteen

NOW THAT MISSY WAS MY responsibility, Mark and I started searching for a suitable chimpanzee sanctuary.

We first started with South Africa, not only because that is my homeland, but also because the wildlife sanctuaries there are among the best in the world.

First prize, we decided, would be getting her into a fantastic reserve called Chimp Eden, near Barberton in the Mpumalanga province. It specializes in rescue and care for chimps either in need of refuge or those that have been victims of the bushmeat trade.

In other words, chimpanzees like Missy.

I tracked down their contact details as I also wanted to find out what Missy should be eating as a premium diet and the exact quotas of milk formula she needed. It had all been a bit hit and miss at the farm so far, giving her milk and whatever fruit I could get. And judging by her condition when I was away, I suspected as times she wasn't fed anything at all.

Chimp Eden is part of the prestigious Jane Goodall Institute, and the sanctuary manager, Phillip Cronje, was a huge help. He outlined optimal milk quotas and what she should eat, and it was also a great comfort knowing I now had professional advice just a phone call away.

I then I asked Phillip the million-dollar question: Was there any possibility that Chimp Eden could take Missy in? Did they have room for her?

That was what was really on my mind.

His reply was cautiously positive. But he said he had to get the board to agree first.

Now that she was with us fulltime, Missy required constant attention. She still wasn't happy being put into a cot on her own at night so she continued sleeping in our bed, latched onto me. I was the first to admit that she had me wrapped around her lanky finger, but in the wild a baby chimp clings to its mother until it is weaned, and is always surrounded by family. I was now, in her eyes, her family.

In fact, her mother.

After a few days with us Missy's health was completely restored and she was thriving. I think for the first time in her life she had a fulltime foster parent and I relished that role.

Mark was an absolute saint, as having Missy attached to me most of the time wasn't the most romantic scenario. Indeed, she was attached even in our intimate moments.

In the evenings she would hang onto me, even if it meant she had to endure getting a bit wet while I was in the bath or having a shower. Sometimes I managed to give her a wash as well without too much of a fuss. That was usually in the day so that after a toweling-off she could dry quickly in the hot sun.

Sometimes, when she had fallen asleep, I managed to gently pull her off and tiptoe to the bathroom to have a sneaky but welcome wash on my own. But if Missy happened to wake up and see I wasn't there, all hell would break loose. She would start with a low, pitiful cry, which quickly crescendoed to a scream. I made sure I was never more than several steps away so I could be with her instantly to pick her up before she started panicking too much.

All the while, we waited for Chimp Eden's decision.

My anxiety at getting her into the sanctuary as soon as possible was aggravated after I met an expat at a supermarket who had heard of Missy and told me she had also rescued a chimp. Unlike Missy, it wasn't a baby – about five years old – but unfortunately it became so destructive that her husband had to build a cage outside for it.

That was the last thing I wanted and told her that Missy was hopefully going to a sanctuary in South Africa.

The woman shook her head; that was a route she had also already unsuccessfully been down. No sanctuary she had

100

approached would take her chimp, and thus she had no choice but to keep it with her in Liberia. Even worse, she and her husband were scheduled to leave the country soon and she had no idea what to do with the chimp, or what would happen to it, when they had gone. I empathized with her dilemma, but felt sorrier for the chimp she rescued and wondered why Liberia had no sanctuary for such animals.

A week later I got the best news in the world. Chimp Eden's board had reviewed Missy's situation. The answer was 'yes'. The sanctuary would take her in.

We were ecstatic. Things were going well. Maybe too well.

Phillip told me the sanctuary also had a young male chimpanzee about the same age as Missy, who would be her companion. The best way we could guess Missy's age was by the growth of her teeth, indicating she was about ten months old. Phillip said that was the approximate age of their other chimp. It would be wonderful for both to have a playmate their own age.

However, that would only come with time, as Missy would be in quarantine for three months once she arrived at the sanctuary.

A typical Monrovian suburb and (below) Missy in
the bathroom basin

Gail carrying Missy 'African-style'

Gail and Missy. (Below) Yekapa Nimba County – encroachment
is a growing threat to chimp habitat

Missy, undernourished on our return from South Africa

Missy holding Mark's hand at the farm

Fifteen

I WAS NOW IN A ROUTINE with my new toddler, and believe me, I don't have children but I'm pretty sure looking after a baby chimp is just as demanding.

Missy would wake up early, usually around 6 a.m. bursting with energy like most tots. First she had her milk and then would start bouncing around the bed, followed by nipping Mark's toes and nose, not necessarily in that order. That usually got his attention. For her, this was the most fun in the world.

Next it was breakfast and then more playtime – this time thankfully off the bed and outside.

Our apartment was the only one with a private patio at the back, which was built around a majestic tree that was perfect as a makeshift jungle gym. One of the gardeners tied a thick rope on a branch, knotting it every few inches for grips so she could climb up and down. He then tied another rope which just hung loosely, which she could swing freely like she would in the jungle.

At first she wouldn't let go of me to climb the ropes, but with a little patience, curiosity got the better of her. Then her hardwired primate instincts kicked in and she realized how much fun this climbing lark could be.

However, she always checked that I was within an arm's reach.

The garden furniture, consisting of a simple table and chairs, became another improvised jungle gym, and swinging on an armrest provided hours of fun.

The downside of this was that Missy regularly disturbed spiders that seemed to cluster under the table, which promptly came scurrying out heading straight for me. I'm an arachnophobe, so you can imagine the results – much shrieking and undignified karaoke to try and get the horrid creepy-crawlies off me.

However, when that happened, Missy thought I was about to abandon her and yelled for me to pick her up. Which gave me two options; either continue trying to get rid of the spiders on me; or pick Missy up knowing that she might have some on her as well.

Talk about a rock and a hard place.

Late afternoons, when Mark got home from work, we would invariably go down to the swimming pool. He would have a swim, then we would relax at the poolside, reveling in the magnificent view of the Atlantic and beautiful sunsets.

Some days Mark would take a rod or hand line to fish in the sea. Missy and I would go with him and sit on the beach, where, just like a human toddler, she loved to play in the sand.

By now Mark was up to his neck in sorting out all the legal hoops we had to jump through to get Missy to South Africa. It was quite a process as the law in Liberia stipulates that no chimpanzee may leave the country without authorization and a motivated scenario.

Then once that avalanche of paperwork was done, a Veterinary Surgeon and an assistant would have to fly to Liberia to take blood samples for various potential diseases, AIDs and Ebola being two key ones.

However, this was further complicated as South African law stated that only a vet from South Africa or the United Kingdom could do this. The blood would be flown to Holland for testing, and then an approximate 10-day wait for the results. All of this would be at our expense. (Mark learnt quickly that shopping isn't my weakness – spending money on animals is.)

From the start, getting the relevant paperwork was a tedious, frustrating procedure. The Catch 22 was that South Africa needed the import CITES (Convention on International Trade of Endangered Species) document to start the ball rolling, while Liberia needed the export CITES document to do so. One could not be started without the other.

So we couldn't begin the export process without having the import documents. But the only way to get the import documents was to have the export papers. It was a classic chicken and egg scenario.

In trying to sort this out, Mark was in contact with a Mr. Francisco at the Department of Agriculture, and they formed a good relationship. Mr. Francisco agreed that as there was no sanctuary for chimps in Liberia, it was in Missy's best interests to be sent elsewhere.

Consequently, he arranged for us to speak to the Forest Development Authority (FDA), which would be responsible for issuing the CITES export permit. Assuming it was just another technicality, we weren't too worried when we arrived at the FDA offices to meet the relevant official.

After introducing ourselves we gave a brief story as to how we acquired Missy and where she would be going.

I was relaxed, thinking the official would rubberstamp everything.

Instead I got the shock of my life. The exact opposite happened. Missy would not be allowed out of the country under any circumstances, he said.

What? The expression on our faces said it all.

In fact, the official continued, he had just returned from a primate summit in Paris where it was agreed that Liberia, in accordance with a global initiative to preserve the greater ape species, could not sign any CITES export document whatsoever.

This, according to him, meant that Missy would not be able to leave Liberia – ever!

I reeled back in astonishment. I could not believe what I was hearing. How could this suddenly happen when everything was going so well?

We left, dumbfounded. On the way home Mark phoned Phillip at Chimp Eden to relay the devastating news.

However, Phillip didn't seem too concerned and said that there were exceptions to this ruling. He would get hold of the FDA to explain the exceptions and assist with the necessary export documentation.

This provided at least a glimmer of hope. With Mark's calm reassurance, I cooled down.

Mark refused even to consider defeat. While waiting for Phillip to get the 'exceptions' sorted out, he was busy with other major logistics that we would face in getting Missy to – hopefully – her new home.

First he wrote to the CEO of South African Airways asking for assistance in flying Missy to South Africa, explaining that this could be a wonderful public relations exercise in giving an orphaned endangered species infant a new life.

There was no reply. So he approached Kenya Airways, presenting them with the same feel-good marketing campaign to sponsor Missy's transport.

The responses were as different as day and night. Kenya Airways were polite, enthusiastic and responded right away. They liked the campaign and agreed to transport Missy to her new home.

More positive news was that the courier company DHL also agreed to sponsor getting Missy's blood samples to Holland, while the Blood Bank would sponsor the actual tests.

With Phillip's knowledge of the legalities, the FDA soon had the necessary paperwork to allay their concerns, and we had our CITES export documents from Liberia.

All the jigsaw pieces were at last falling into place.

With the CITES export document now sorted out, we submitted the CITES import document. This had to be approved by the South African authorities.

In the interim, Phillip suggested that Missy should spend some time with other caregivers to ease her stress of leaving me. I agreed that was a good idea, but it tore at my heart knowing that Missy would soon be losing another mother figure.

We decided that task should be given to Annie, who so far had been really good with Missy. Annie was happy to take on that role, so Missy would now spend an increasing amount of time with her to get used to other people.

But this had to be done gradually as Missy threw major tantrums if I was not within a meter or two of her. So Mark and I decided to get Annie to babysit for about half an

112

hour each weekday. We could increase this as Missy, hopefully, grew more comfortable with the arrangement.

I knew we had to do this for Missy's good, although I hated being away from her. On the plus side, I suppose, it gave me some time to have a swim on my own.

As usual, this was far easier said than done. I would hand her over to Annie and then dash out the door as soon as Missy started screaming. She would yell so loud that I could hear her all the way from the swimming pool. It upset me terribly.

After a few minutes she would usually calm down. When I returned to the apartment I often found her asleep – but I learnt this was purely from the exhaustion of throwing a massive hissy fit.

If she was awake, she would make a huge racket when she saw me again, reaching out for me to pick her up. There was no doubt that her comfort zone was on my hip with my arms around her.

So life went on while the snail-speed wheels of bureaucracy continued grinding.

Apart from the half hour with Annie each day, Missy and I were inseparable. I knew our time together was short and that her attachment to me may not be in her best interests, but there was nothing I could do in the interim.

In her eyes, I was her mother. Her short-term need was that I take care of her as best I could. I had already made that vow when I first saw her at the farm during our visit with Sydney and David. I was not going to renege on that.

She came with me everywhere; the beach, the pool, even grocery shopping, where she was quite a handful. I often underestimated the length of her arms and if I walked past something of interest, she simply grabbed it from the shelf, resulting in me having hurriedly to put unwanted merchandise back before being charged for it.

On most expeditions to the supermarkets she was the star attraction among other shoppers and staff. When that happened, I got onto my soapbox stressing to all and sundry that Missy was not a pet. She was with me temporarily until we could find a sanctuary. A wild animal should never be as a pet, I kept repeating.

If I managed to convert a few people, then all that verbal energy will have been worth it. I sincerely hope I did.

Some chores I could only do by putting Missy on my back, wrapped around with a sarong, African-style. This gave me use of both hands – until Missy figured she could wiggle out of the sarong.

Missy, of course, was also comfortable and happy to be with Mark. He was the playful, fun foster dad, I was the overprotective, serious mother figure.

Like all juvenile chimps, Missy loved to be tickled. I never knew that baby chimps are ticklish like human toddlers. A chimp has an infectious, unique laugh. Mark would tickle her and she would take his hand and place it behind her neck for more. It was the most delightful engagement to watch.

114

Sometimes I thought she would run out of breath she laughed so much.

Her delightful intrusion in my everyday life was total. She loved exploring my handbag, and if my makeup purse was open, out came that as well. She was an enchanting prima donna, and I still smile when I remember all this.

Each morning, as I was putting on makeup or brushing my teeth, Missy would clamber up the basin with the agility and grace of a circus acrobat. She would grab the toilet paper holder as her first rung and then use the momentum to grasp the lip of the basin to swing herself up.

For her, everything was new and wildly interesting and exciting. It took me twice as long to get ready each morning as not only did I have to watch Missy's every move, I also had to put on makeup and brush my teeth with a fascinated chimp swinging around the bathroom.

If she was not wondering what I was doing, she was pulling towels off the rack and dragging them around on the floor after her.

I also was amazed at her impressive strength; she could push over a large plastic chair with ease, something a human baby could never do.

It was not always that carefree, unfortunately. One morning while I was in the bathroom, Missy grabbed the toilet pipe and with a yank disconnected it. It was so quick that by the time I noticed what was happening, it was too late.

The next instant the loose pipe was writhing like a swishing snake, spraying everything in range – including me.

I grabbed it, but Missy got such a fright that she jumped squealing onto my now-soaked back.

Not knowing what to do, I jammed the squirting pipe into the toilet, closed the seat top and dashed for my phone.

"Annie, please get here!"

Poor Annie rushed into the bathroom to find absolute chaos.

Missy was clinging onto my back, while I was kneeling holding the pipe still twisting like a demented serpent down the toilet. Both of us were drenched from head to foot.

Annie took the pipe from me while pointing to the water valve where I promptly turned off the water.

She then called Tyrus, the handyman, while I toweled Missy down and changed out of my sopping clothes.

We mopped the bathroom, finishing just minutes before Tyrus knocked at the door.

Annie showed him where the pipe broke, thankfully making no mention of Missy actually yanking it out.

He nodded in sympathy, saying yes, the pipe was rusty and he was not surprised it snapped. He would fix it in no time. It was not our fault

All the while Missy sat quietly on my hip, holding onto me with the face of an angel.

Tyrus never found out what really happened.

Sixteen

O UR TWO FRIENDS CALLED FADI, who had rescued Charlie the African Grey parrot, invited us to meet them one evening at the Golden Beach for an impromptu early dinner.

We joined them at their table and after greeting the men, Missy promptly fell asleep.

A few minutes later a woman walked past our table, saw Missy dozing in my lap, and looked at me with utter disgust.

"Do you know what you are doing? Do you realize chimpanzees are an endangered species? You have absolutely no right to keep a baby!" she blurted out.

I was taken aback, but quickly recovered.

"Before you jump down my throat, perhaps you should hear me out first!" was my equally animated reply.

I told her how we happened to have Missy in our care and her pending relocation to a sanctuary in South Africa.

In no way, I stressed, did we regard her as a pet.

That broke the ice and I soon discovered I had found my match – an equally crazy animal lover called Phoebe McKinney.

She was an American and we exchanged phone numbers, promising to get together to brainstorm on how to do some charity work for the thousands of animals in need in Liberia.

Mark and the two Fadis guffawed delightedly at this fiery-turned-friendly clash. Mark said that if the roles had been reversed with Phoebe sitting with a chimp on her lap, my 'Monster Moment' would have erupted and I would have gone on the attack just as she had. Maybe even more so.

How right they were! I was being given a taste of my own medicine. And it was good to know that there were other people like me out there. It was not long before Phoebe and I became friends. She would play a major role in helping us out later.

Back in our apartment, ever-ingenious Mark discovered that the security bars outside our window could be another improvised jungle gym for Missy by the simple expedient of sliding the window open. It was a great idea and provided hours of fun. She would climb to the top of the couch, then reach for one of the bars and hoist herself up.

Once up, she would show off her gymnastic skills, which sometimes were a little too daring and tangled my nerves up in knots. I was certain she was going to slip and fall during some of her more audacious moves.

But climbing was fused in her genes. I had to keep reminding myself that – hey, this was what chimps do.

Her acrobatic display also provided great entertainment for anyone walking or driving past our apartment, who invariably stopped to watch. I think Missy often played to the crowd. She oozed mischievous charm, and had also learnt to take off her diaper, which proved to be a lot easier when she was climbing. She would hold onto the burglar bars with one hand and energetically yank at the nappy with the other. Then she would simply step out of the cumbersome garb when it reached her knees.

By now she had learnt what 'no' meant, and knew that taking off her diaper was going to get her a stern reprimand – if I managed not to laugh that is. But she considered that worth the scolding.

A few of the expats asked if I was worried that she would jump off the security bars and run away. I shook my head. That would not happen.

In fact, the opposite was true – Missy kept checking that I was still there, not the other way around. She was more scared of me leaving than I was of her running off. If I even casually stood up, she would immediately slide down the bars and jump onto the couch, shrilly voicing a terror that perhaps only someone who has seen her own mother slaughtered could voice. She was petrified that I was going off without her.

Simon, the compound gardener was particularly intrigued by her. While tending to Mark's small herb and vegetable garden by the patio, he said he never realized how much chimps were like humans.

For Simon, this was a completely alien concept; a 'buboon' acting like a human? He had never in his wildest dreams believed that creatures of the jungle also had characters and were individuals. To him they were just bushmeat.

Missy completely reversed that. Every day he would greet her and watch, fascinated, as she interacted with me. He soon became very fond of her and promised that he would share how wonderful, loving and intelligent chimpanzees were with his community.

In fact, he went further – he pledged to teach his people to respect and look after the animals that are being ruthlessly slaughtered to extinction. For me, this was a massive breakthrough. If more people thought like that, the bushmeat trade and selling of orphaned wild animals to well-meaning but gullible people would be something shameful from the past.

Missy had become an ambassador for her fellow chimps. Okay, it was only on a tiny scale. But that's where you have to start.

Mark and I had another trip planned to South Africa at the end of January. By this time Missy and I were inseparable. She didn't want me to go anywhere without her and made that very clear. As we found out on one particularly hot Sunday afternoon when one of our friends, Emily Tarr, offered to hold Missy so that I could have a dip in the pool with Mark.

I had only swum a length when I saw that Emily was having a tough time controlling Missy, who kept trying to get to me. With just my head exposed, as quietly as I could, I told Emily that I was about to get out and take Missy back.

Unfortunately, Missy heard my voice and this set her off even more, frantically struggling to get to me.

Emily held her tight and got bitten for her troubles. Thankfully, she understood that the bite was purely reflexive as Missy was in a flat spin. Fortunately, the wound was superficial.

Mark and I couldn't cancel our trip to South Africa, so we decided to shorten it from two weeks to just one, as we had in December. But trying to find a babysitter for Missy while we were away, was not easy.

Most expats who were willing to babysit worked during the day, while the few that didn't have jobs weren't too comfortable handling a baby chimpanzee.

I also didn't want her to be around children for her own sake as well as that of any child. Children can be a Petri dish of germs, and in turn they would be more susceptible than adults to getting a bug from Missy. I couldn't risk her biting a child either. Apart from Emily, so far Missy had also nipped Mark, David and Annie.

A Liberian woman named Betty was the main babysitter at the compound. She worked for Fadi Chdid and had previously babysat his two young children before they had left to go to school back home in Lebanon. Betty was an ideal candidate as her own children were grown up and she knew Missy and was comfortable with her.

Fadi was also great, saying Betty could bring Missy with her when she came to clean his apartment for part of the day.

What a relief. We had a babysitter.

Betty would be taking Missy home with her after work, so for my own peace of mind, I wanted to see where Missy would be staying. Betty's home was in a typical Liberian village, except the houses were not traditional African huts. There were scattered around a clearing, and although all were close to each other, there no walls or barriers separating them.

It seemed fine for Missy as Betty promised to keep the baby chimp with her at all times. Betty's neighbors were also very friendly, especially the children who were eager to greet me.

The plan was that Betty and Annie would take turns babysitting Missy during the day, while at night she would go home with Betty. We organized a taxi in advance to fetch and drop Bettie and Missy off at the compound each morning and then take them back home in the afternoon.

I also stocked up with plenty of fruit, milk and bottled water, which Peter delivered to Betty's home.

It goes without saying that while in South Africa I phoned Betty every morning for updates. She was superb, giving me detailed feedback on how much milk Missy had drunk, what fruit she liked, how and where she slept and what she did for fun.

Our visit home went quickly, thanks to a hectic schedule, and it was fantastic catching up with all our loved ones. However, Missy was always on my mind. I couldn't wait to get back to her.

She was now such a part of my life that I felt lost without her.

Returning to Liberia to find a happy, well-looked-after Missy was a massive relief. In just a week Missy had bonded beautifully with Betty – unlike our previous trip when Missy had been left at the farm and got injured by a donkey.

We also bought the perfect gift for her from South Africa; a fluffy, lifelike, toy chimpanzee. It was just a little bigger than she was, although that wouldn't be for long at the rate Missy was growing. I couldn't wait to see her reaction to it.

It was a huge hit. Missy bonded with her new fluffy friend at first sight. We named it Mogli and within minutes

Missy was throwing it into her cot, then jumping in and diving on top of it.

Sometimes Mogli got a kiss and sometimes a slap in the face. You never knew what was coming next. However, Missy was quite jealous of her new friend and didn't like Mogli getting any attention from Mark and me.

Some nights I managed to trick Missy into falling asleep in her own cot. I placed it on two chairs so that it would be the same height as the bed and then lay next to her until she was almost asleep. Once she was snoozing, I would gently move her over to the cot next to Mogli to give her something to cling onto.

With only Annie and Bettie as alternate babysitters, Missy spent most of her time with me. She was comfortable with the other two women, but there was no doubt that I was the 'mother'.

Even though it was now a daily ritual to hand her over to Annie to give me a short break, whenever that happened she would frantically yell, scrambling to get back to me. She would soon settle down though.

It was the same with Bettie, although we generally only used her to babysit for us on Sundays.

Somehow word got out that I was an animal Samaritan and locals started coming to the compound to try and get me to buy other wild animals. Every now and again I would be called to the gates by the security guards and outside would be a man holding some trussed-up creature.

It was heartbreaking. I had to send them away. I hated it as I knew that the animal would most likely die.

All I could do was sternly tell whoever brought the animal that what they were doing was wrong. Wild animals are never meant to be kept as pets. They are called 'wild' for a reason.

Besides, as I kept stressing, even if I had the space to take an animal in it would just result in hunters going back and catching another one after shooting its parents for bushmeat.

Maybe I did not change anyone's mind, although I hope so.

But at least I was putting the record straight.

Seventeen

ON OUR NEXT VISIT TO THE farm, we stopped at the gate so Adele could say hello to Missy. She was stunned to see how much Missy had grown and how well she looked.

She put her arms out to take her, but Missy was having none of that. She made it very clear that she was not leaving my side.

The golf course Mark was building was fast taking shape. We drove over and many of the workers came across to see Missy, also commenting on how much she had grown and how healthy she was.

Then the farm manager came over to say hello and told me that Missy had screamed for two days when we left her with Jonathan while we were in South Africa over Christmas. I was not surprised, remembering the condition Missy had been in when we returned. She obviously had pined for us terribly.

Soon afterwards, Mark woke one morning not feeling well. Most bugs don't deter Mark from going to work, and flu or other ailments that keep the rest of us in bed are shrugged off by his stubborn will to get things done.

However, this time even he was flattened. He didn't even want to speak to anyone. I tried to get him to go to see a doctor, but this was brushed off with the curt comment that all he needed was a day's rest.

No amount of nagging would persuade him otherwise, although he did vaguely promise me that he would go to the doctor first thing the following morning.

That didn't ease my apprehension as in West Africa, where malaria is endemic, you don't delay any visit to a doctor.

By evening Mark had taken a turn for the worse. He now had a nasty fever. A few of our friends shared my concerns and John, one of the compound owners, said he would personally take Mark to the doctor the next day.

The following morning Mark barely had the energy or the will to get dressed. True to his word, John arrived early, bundled Mark into his car and off they went. Mark assured me that I needn't go with.

Blood test results told the grim story; Mark not only had malaria, but typhoid as well. Thankfully Liberia is well equipped to deal with both diseases as they are extremely common in that part of the world.

But even by Liberian standards, this was really serious. Mark spent the next three days on a drip and my strong-as-an-ox Fox was man-down for two weeks. You have to know Mark to grasp how unusual that is for him.

Not long after leaving his sick bed, he got more devastating news. Arriving at the office one morning in early March, he was coldly informed that another distribution company was taking over the running of his division.

Which meant that he was out of a job.

It was a bombshell. There was no way we could have seen this coming. In fact, the opposite was true. Mark got on very well with Jack, his boss, and was repeatedly told that apart from his strong performance at his day job, he was doing great work in finishing off the golf course on Jack's farm.

Even more confusing was the fact that the owner of the company replacing Mark's division did not have the reputation of being a respected man in Liberia. He had made a fortune in the country, but was not universally liked. Or so we were told.

This was a real kick in the teeth for Mark as he had worked hard and had reaped good rewards for the company. He had more than doubled revenue since he had taken over the previous year.

To add insult to injury, his January salary check had bounced and he hadn't been paid for February. The company also hadn't paid rent for our apartment at Ocean View as it was contractually bound to do. An apartment in a gated compound in Liberia is extremely expensive, and to keep ours Mark now had to pay the rent out of his own pocket.

However, being the eternal optimist that he is, Mark had faith that he would get the pay he was entitled to and that this was just an oversight. He believed the culprit was one of the company's partners, a man who was feared by a lot of Liberians. Once the senior partner intervened, Mark believed it would be sorted out.

Fortunately, we still had the use of the company car which we definitely needed.

The future, for better or worse, was now clear. With Mark's contract coming to an abrupt end, we now had no choice but to leave Liberia.

The one thing holding us back, of course, was Missy. We could not just abandon her, which sadly often happened to chimps rescued by expats when they left. We decided that as soon as she was on her way to Chimp Eden in South Africa, we would also pack up and go home.

As far as Missy's move was concerned, things were going reasonably well. We had most of the paperwork done, so now it was just a waiting game. Phillip told us we would have to hang on for the application to reach the top of the pile. He could not expedite that, despite our rather unexpected change of circumstances.

With our imminent departure looming, we made the most of every day. I was sad that we were going to be leaving Liberia prematurely, and I certainly was going to miss the fun and pleasures of life as an expat. I had also hoped to get more involved with helping animals in need in the country, something I had discussed with my friend and fellow animal-lover Phoebe. Obviously that now was not going to happen.

We were also going to miss all the good friends we had made and, of course, living right next to the sea – something neither of us had ever done before. But the long wet season was about to kick off and the nasty tropical diseases that incubate during the incessant rains were two good reasons to depart before summer started.

It also, of course, would be great to see our friends and family back home. Liberia had been a fantastic adventure, but the fact it was about to end was beyond our control. We had no choice but to move on.

We decided we had to be gone by the end of April.

Then came Ebola.

Eighteen

AROUND MID-MARCH, HEADLINES splashed across newspapers, TV and radio bulletins around the country trumpeted the news that a man in neighboring Guinea had died from Ebola.

Despite the widespread publicity, it did not raise any major alarms at the time; just sympathy for dead man's family.

A couple of days later a few more Ebola deaths in Guinea were reported. Again, there was no panic as Guinea was far away from Monrovia.

However, local radio stations were now broadcasting that the authorities were cautioning Liberians not to cross the border into Guinea unless they had to.

In other words, most people were aware that there was an outbreak of the deadly virus in a neighboring country, but it was still relatively isolated. There was no indication whatsoever of a looming epidemic.

Or so we thought. Then came the report we were dreading; a Liberian was diagnosed with Ebola in the Lofa district, which borders Guinea in the north.

Overnight, the situation changed. With a local person infected, it was getting closer to home. Liberians were now being told not to eat bushmeat and to stay away from 'buboons' (baboons and chimpanzees) and monkeys. Ebola causes hemorrhagic fever in humans and other primates, including chimps, and I couldn't help thinking that as awful as the killer disease was, it would at least temporarily curb the bushmeat slaughter.

From then on, it started escalating with more Ebola deaths being reported each day, both in Guinea and now increasingly in Liberia.

Then a man died from Ebola at Firestone, which is about 40 minutes by car from Monrovia. The virus had suddenly leapfrogged several hundred kilometers and was nearing the capital's perimeter.

Soon Ebola was the dreaded word on everyone's lips. Its ghostly specter haunted the entire country. There were those who were afraid, those who were angry that they were told to refrain from eating bushmeat and, bizarrely, those who believed that America had somehow manufactured the virus and let it loose to kill West Africans.

This paranoia now starting to affect us directly. With the repeated warnings to stay away from chimpanzees and widespread ignorance of how Ebola is actually spread, some of the expats in our compound began looking warily at Missy.

She could be a carrier, they said, despite the fact that this was impossible as she'd had no contact whatsoever with the disease.

A few panic-stricken expats cornered the compound owners, John and Luke, saying that Missy was a serious health hazard and must be evicted immediately.

I could not believe it. This was horrifying; if the educated expats believed Missy was a deadly risk, what would ordinary Liberians, without the benefits of much education think? Thanks to the descent into hell during the lengthy civil wars, Liberia was sadly one of the most undeveloped countries in the world.

As the paranoia grew wings and spread, John told Mark about some of the expats' concerns and stressed we should keep Missy inside at all times.

We obliged. I think John was on our side but he had no choice except to listen to the other tenants. He had a business to run, and you cannot run a business with panicky customers.

I phoned Chimp Eden in South Africa to ask Phillip for more detailed information on Ebola. He had heard about the outbreak in West Africa and told me Missy would have already died if she had been exposed to it before we took her in. The fact that she was healthy meant that she was absolutely no threat at all.

Chimpanzees are not a host of the virus as many people wrongly believe. In fact, three species of fruit bats are thought to be carriers, although a chimpanzee can catch Ebola from fruit eaten by infected bats.

Also, Ebola incubation is between two and 21 days. The fact that Missy had been with us in an Ebola-free environment for longer than that also proved that she was not at risk.

Phillip sent me internet links with info on the virus, which quelled my growing fears. Despite this, I will never forget him saying, "Missy will still be blamed for many things."

Instinctively, I knew that was a prophecy. The truth does not always protect the innocent.

Then Annie walked in the apartment on the Tuesday morning looking very worried,

"Ev'rybod' afrai' Missy hav' Ebol'," she said. "Many of de expats not happy she here."

Then Annie said something that chilled me to the bone.

"I too scare' she ha' Ebol'."

If even Annie thought Missy was infected, what would we do next?

I immediately assured her that Missy was no threat, explaining as best as I could what Phillip had told me. The main thing to understand, I said, was that if Missy had been exposed to Ebola, she would already be dead. I then printed off some of the articles from the internet and gave them to her to read.

Annie trusted us implicitly and accepted my explanation, which was a huge relief. She had been with us long enough to know that we would never put other people's lives at risk if there was even the slightest possibility that Missy was infected. We really needed her on our side.

Then Peter said he was worried. That too was a huge shock as Peter was not just an employee – he was a friend who like Annie had been with us for the entire duration of my stay in the country. I did my best to reassure him and, as with Annie, it didn't take me long. He knew that we would also be putting our own lives as risk if Missy was a threat.

Soon after that even a few of our close expat friends were suddenly avoiding us. It was obvious that they were afraid of being near Missy.

This was getting really serious. We had to get Missy to South Africa as soon as humanly possible.

There was no question about that.

Nineteen

IT WASN'T EASY KEEPING MISSY, with her boundless energy, confined inside the apartment.

For a start, her favorite pastime was climbing up and down the burglar guards. This she would do in full view of other tenants, some of whom had already expressed concerns that she was an Ebola time-bomb just waiting to explode. Obviously we could no longer let her do that.

I tried to distract her with other activities, inwardly seething at people's ignorance. She was so obviously a healthy baby chimp, and instead of rallying around to help her and let an endangered wild animal have a decent shot at life, we instead had to 'jail' her.

It also was confusing for Missy. She couldn't understand why I suddenly no longer let her climb on the burglar bars.

Thankfully, I was still able to take her outside at the back patio so that she could get some fresh air and climb the ropes on the tree. As this was relatively private, she would not be easily seen. The only person regularly coming around the back was Simon the gardener, who watered our herbs.

I had to get Simon on board immediately. When I next saw him, I wasted no time in taking him aside and telling him the facts about chimps and Ebola. The main thing I had to convince him of was that Missy was absolutely risk-free.

I also showed him the articles I had printed off the internet.

Simon nodded and agreed not to tell anyone when Missy was playing outside on the patio. He trusted us and accepted my word that Missy was not a threat, and I think he was relieved to do so. He had grown hugely fond of his little friend, as he used to call her.

However, like Missy I was also getting cabin fever. I hadn't left the apartment for close on a week.

Ebola paranoia – justifiably so in most instances – now gripped the entire country. At the compound, all staff were ordered by management to wash their hands after going into each and every apartment. Any staff member who felt even mildly off-color, was told in no uncertain terms told to stay at home.

In fact, all physical contact was considered a risk, which was a problem as Liberians are a remarkably tactile people. Shaking hands is a respectful and traditional way of saying hello, although not in the Western sense. A Liberian handshake is a rite in itself, a clasp of hands then a click of the fingers, something I was never able to master.

But now in the fear and loathing of Ebola-stricken Liberia, even shaking hands was considered to be life-threatening.

Other inherent dangers included eating fruit and vegetables bought from the market. Only locally grown food with a thick skin like a banana was considered safe.

Some of the expats left the country in a flat panic, and who could blame them? We were about to leave ourselves, although not because of Ebola. But we certainly were not going to leave until we knew for certain that Missy would be safely cared for.

Then Annie told me some expats were terrified of being near anyone, let alone a chimpanzee. They said they didn't want their apartments cleaned by local people anymore.

There was also big drama when one of the Ocean View cleaners had a miscarriage and the expat she worked for refused to allow her into the apartment.

Miscarriages are a side effect of Ebola. In this case, the premature loss of the baby was just a tragedy many women suffer and had nothing to do with the killer virus. But even so, you had to be there to understand the dread that was running rampant everywhere.

One morning I had no choice but to go shopping as we had run out of vital supplies. The supermarket resembled a sci-fi movie set. All the cashiers and staff wore gloves and masks. It was just like being served by Michael Jackson.

By now Ebola terror permeated every aspect of all our lives. In a country where most communication relies on little more than a rudimentary gossip grapevine, the Ebola threat had reached the highest level of Code Red that you can imagine. Everyone, not only jungle animals, was suspected of being an Ebola incubator.

Even I felt stirs of panic at the absolute craziness sweeping the country – and I knew for an absolute scientific certainty that Ebola is not an airborne virus. It can only be transmitted by physical contact.

One morning I noticed Missy had boil-like sores on her face and neck. I had changed her milk formula when the brand she was weaned on had sold out at all shops, so initially I thought the cause could have been the change of diet.

Soon one of the sores on her lip started to grow rapidly, disfiguring her face. Missy scratched at it, which aggravate the pustule. I phoned Phillip to ask for advice and emailed a photograph. Phillip said he would get back to me, but in the interim he suggested I fortify her diet with vitamin supplements and rub antibacterial cream onto the 'boils'.

When even more pustules developed, I still wasn't overly concerned as Missy was full of beans and as vigorous as an athlete. Apart from incessantly scratching at her sores, she looked the picture of health.

The next day, when I had her on my lap and was about to rub cream on her, to my horror I saw the pustule start to quiver.

Then, as I watched aghast, a worm popped out, just like in a B-grade horror flick. I phoned Mark in a panic saying, "There's a horrible worm crawling out of Missy's boil. What should I do?"

"Phone Phillip," Mark calmly replied.

Phillip listened to my semi-garbled description and had just received a probable diagnosis from a sanctuary in Sierra Leone, who said it could be maggots from the tumbu fly, or putzi, as they are more commonly known.

So all these pustules meant that Missy was riddled with maggots? That sounded really gross. I then scrutinized another large boil on her mouth. There was movement under the skin there too. Yes – definitely putzi worms.

Phillip said I had no option but to remove the maggots manually myself. I reeled back in horror. Pulling worms out with my hands?

He explained how. All the pustules have microscopic breathing holes. If I smothered the hole with Vaseline, the worms would start to suffocate and squiggle to the surface for air. Then all I had to do was yank the worm out and clean the sore with disinfectant.

Simple, but not exactly great fun.

I sat Missy on my lap, and starting with the maggot on her lip I smeared Vaseline over the hole and waited for the bug to emerge.

It didn't. For half an hour I stared at the pustule, waiting. Nothing happened.

I made another call to Phillip.

"It's not working. They aren't coming out, no matter how much Vaseline I put on.

Phillip gave a quiet chuckle. "No, you have to squeeze them out. I bet you never thought you would ever be squeezing maggots. Just give a firm pinch and make sure the whole thing emerges. If a section is left inside it could cause an infection."

"Got it."

I placed Missy on her back, shaking a little with the first attempt. I dabbed on a smear of Vaseline. The moment I saw the head of the maggot emerge I squeezed, then quickly picked it up with tweezers, put it in tissue and flushed it out down the toilet. Then I cleaned the sore and smeared on antibacterial cream.

They were all over her body, even on one of her fingers. When I had finished squeezing them out on her back, I turned her onto her tummy. She did not flinch. In fact, she was completely relaxed, almost falling asleep at times.

The putzi fly is found in many parts of Africa. It lays eggs in clothing or towels drying outside. Once the material comes into contact with skin, the eggs hatch and the larvae burrows into the body, eventually morphing into a maggot. I knew exactly where these putzis had come from as I had stupidly left Missy's towel outside one morning.

A week later Mark also had boils on his arm, leg and lip. This time I knew exactly what they were. More putzis! In fact, he found four maggots in one arm alone. I laughed, which wasn't quite the reaction he expected.

Saturday was the opening of the driving range at the golf course Mark had project-managed for Jack. A big event was planned and Mark had been extremely busy helping with the final arrangements and marketing. Annie babysat Missy so I could go with him.

It was a success, even with the Ebola fear, which was a relief and a real achievement for Mark. Even so, Ebola cast its evil shadow everywhere. Although people mingled and chatted, there was no physical contact. There were no handshakes, or even worse, a hug. After a few hours I started to get restless without Missy and managed to get a lift back to the apartment with an expat who also lived there.

We relaxed at the apartment for the rest of the weekend. Mark went to the swimming pool, while I stayed inside hiding Missy in case other residents got nervous. I still could not believe even sophisticated expats didn't grasp that you could not catch Ebola from a heathy chimp who has had no contact with the disease.

It wasn't easy for either of us. I felt like a prisoner and I felt guilty that I couldn't accompany Mark outside. The saving grace was that in a couple of weeks Missy would be on a Kenya Airways flight to South Africa.

Well, that was what we thought.

The weekend was barely over when there was a knock at our door. Annie answered. A man was standing there who gave her an envelope. She brought it to me.

Mark was sitting on the patio having his morning coffee.

Standing in the kitchen, I tore open the envelope.

31 March 2014

Dear Mr. Fox

As you are quite aware of the recent virus killer which is affecting the country, most of our tenants are concerned and expressing their collective fear of this issue.

Secondly, we are unable to continuously allow the animal in the environment in keeping our policy that no domestic animal is allowed in the apartment.

We hope that you will do something as quick as possible by relocating the animal and see reason to understand the life-threatened-concerns of other tenants

Many thanks for your prompt understanding in this matter

Management

We now had nowhere to stay. Unless, of course, we got rid of Missy.

But for both of us, that was unthinkable.

Twenty

I BLURTED OUT A FEW EXPLETIVES and handed the letter to Mark.

"We were given permission to keep Missy here. Now saying that no animals are allowed is bullshit. What are we going to do?" I said.

I don't think I have ever felt so despondent.

"Maybe we could ask Luke and John to send a letter to all the expats explaining Missy isn't a threat," was my desperate suggestion.

Mark finished reading the letter and shrugged slightly as he folded it and put it back on the table. His voice was gentle. He knew and understood the situation perfectly.

"Crocodile, everybody is very afraid. This is John and Luke's business. They have to make their tenants their priority concern."

"What are we going to do? Where are we going to find a place to stay? We can't just get rid of Missy."

Mark started working on it right away. He phoned some of our expat friends who lived in another compound.

Unfortunately, that was a non-starter as the compound owner flatly stated that he couldn't accommodate Missy either. No primates would be allowed in the current situation – in fact, on no account would she even be allowed onto the premises. That's how extensive the Ebola paranoia was.

I then phoned Phoebe. She was as shocked as I was at people's ignorance and said she would try to help us to find another place right away.

Then she had a brainwave. "Why don't you phone Rudolph and ask him if you can stay at the Libassa Ecolodge?"

Of course. What a great idea.

I called Rudolph and told him our dilemma, pleading with him that we had nowhere else to go.

Rudolph was superb. He said the lodge was closed during the week, but for me and Missy he would make an exception. We could stay there until Friday morning.

However, I would have to leave before the weekend as he had several bookings and also couldn't risk frightening off clients. No doubt they would be as paranoiac as some of the expats at Ocean View were.

He was right about that. This was not the best time to try and educate people – they would all have a kneejerk reaction with all the hype and false claims being spread about chimps and Ebola. But at least I had somewhere to stay during the week.

"The one problem," said Rudolph, "is that there will only be electricity from about six in the evening until 10 or 11 at night. Then there will be a power blackout."

I shrugged. That would be the least of my concerns.

"Thank you Rudolph! I cannot say that often enough."

The relief at having somewhere to stay with Missy was overwhelming. Rudolph knew that Missy was not a risk as he understood that Ebola is only spread by direct contact, mainly through blood or body fluids. As I kept saying, it is not an airborne disease. Missy had been with us for about four months, so it was pretty obvious she had not been in contact with an Ebola carrier.

But most importantly for me was that as a fellow animal lover, Rudolph completely understood my pain and panic for Missy's well-being.

Despite having a temporary place to stay, I was still in shock over Missy's sudden eviction from Ocean View. This was totally unexpected. I couldn't concentrate on a simple task like packing clothes and other items to take to Eco Lodge.

Fortunately, ever-reliable Annie was there and she helped me get everything ready, also looking after Missy while Peter drove me to the supermarket to get emergency supplies. Without staff or guests at the Ecolodge, the lodge kitchen was closed so I would be living mainly on snack food for the rest of the week. I also stocked up with a plentiful supply of water, diapers, and milk.

Mark then phoned South Africa to explain the latest turn of events and severity of the situation to Phillip at Chimp Eden. He stressed that we needed to get the paperwork completed was now an absolute priority as Missy was no longer safe in Liberia.

Even some of our friends regarded her as a threat to their health. That's how serious it was.

Apartments in Congo Town (above) and Sinkor Road

Missy with a volunteer at the CCC and (below) with Annie

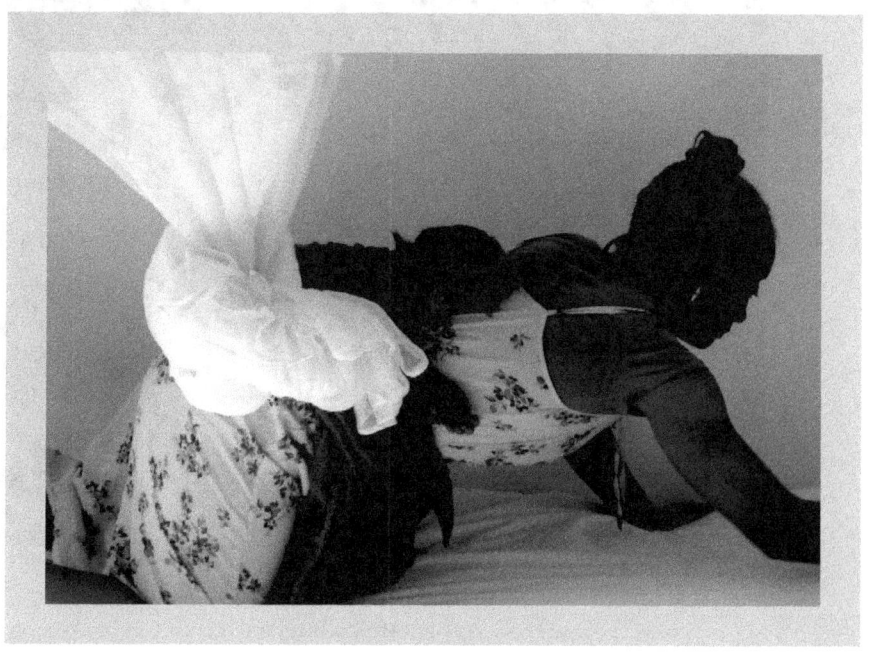

Missy happy travelling with us

Missy – still frail and recovering – with Mark and,
(below) playing with Mogli

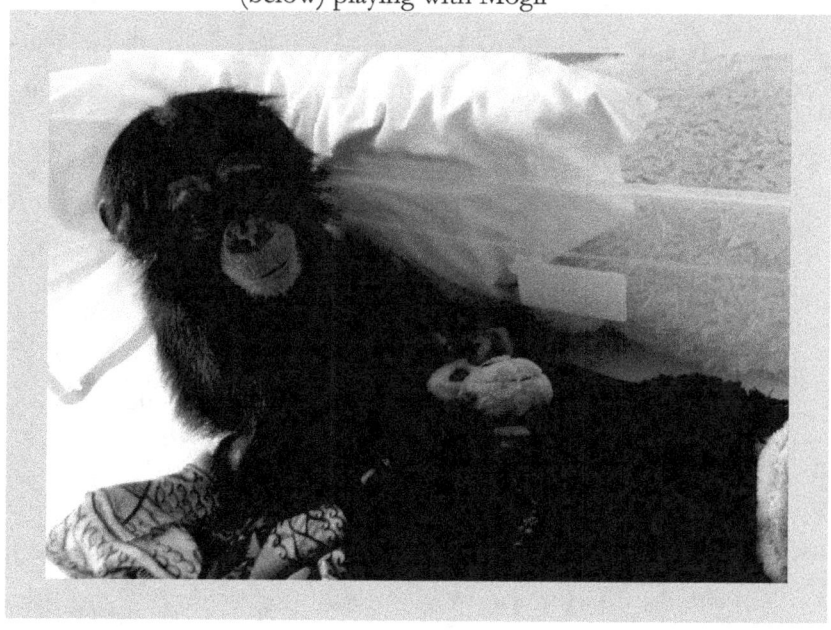

Twenty-One

THE BEAUTIFUL ENTRANCE TO THE Libassa Ecolodge soothed my shattered nerves as I arrived with Missy at what was to be our home for the next few days.

At least she would be in the perfect environment – safe and without any hassles for a change. For the next few days, I would not have to hide her from prying eyes. She was welcome here.

At the entrance Jacob, one of the staff, was waiting for me. He and Peter helped carry my bags to my room, overlooking the swimming pool and dining area right next door to where Mark and I had stayed on a previous visit.

Each room is named after an animal indigenous to Liberia. Missy and I would be staying in the Chimpanzee Room. How apt was that?

Peter had to go back to Monrovia and Jacob treated me like a VIP guest.

154

"Would you like to go to the lagoon?" he said, offering to take me on a tour of the lodge.

I told him that I had been there before, but as this was my most favorite place in Liberia, I would love to have another look.

I followed Jacob through the different pathways that led to the lagoon. He then took me down another path toward the boat house. He was the perfect guide, showing such pride in his country and the piece of paradise that he lived in.

Lastly, he took me to the beach. I didn't want Missy to get too hot, so we had just a short walk, then I returned to my room.

Jacob gave me his cellphone number, "I will be back at six o'clock to put on the generator. If you need anything, you can phone me."

I was exhausted from the heat and the adrenalin rush of the day, so I went inside to have a nap. I had brought Missy's makeshift bed and playpen along, which I put on the main bed.

However, Missy did not share my exhaustion. She took one look at the wooden poles on the four-poster bed and decided straight away that this was the best jungle gym she had ever seen. To her, this was one big glorious adventure and I watched anxiously, hoping she wouldn't break anything.

155

Desperate to get some rest, I gave her Mogli to play with, which she joyously threw over the headboard. This meant that I would have to get up to retrieve the toy chimp, only for it to be tossed over again.

Eventually, after about an hour, she settled down for a nap with me.

Jacob later visited to see if I needed anything and to introduce me to his wife and son. It was getting dark, which in West Africa means mosquito time. Missy and I went back inside.

Mark had an early start the next day so he couldn't spend the night with us. I really missed him. The cell network signal was weak, so even phone calls were hit and miss.

Dusk fell quickly as it always does in the tropics, an eerie silence then darkness which heightened my senses as well as my paranoia of being alone. Soon afterwards the generators were switched off and I couldn't see a thing.

I struggled to sleep and kept visualizing jungle intruders creeping into my room. I knew I was being silly, but I couldn't help myself. My ears pricked up at any slight noise, real or otherwise. Despite myself, my imagination was running riot.

I finally dozed off. Then woke with a start. There was a tap-tap-tap on the window. I sat up in alarm, heart pounding furiously. To my horror I saw a silhouette behind the curtain.

156

Petrified that someone was on the patio stalking me, I had no choice but to pull myself together and check it out. I quietly slipped off the bed and leopard-crawled to the glass door, hoping Missy wouldn't stir. I gently eased the bottom corner of the curtain aside, trying to quell the thumping of my heart, and peered out of the window.

It was the reflection of a tree.

As I climbed back onto the bed, using my cellphone as a flashlight, Missy woke up. It was close to midnight and I sent Mark a message about how fearful I was which I knew would prompt him to call. I figured that if I stood on the bed I would managed to get some sort of network signal and we could speak.

It worked. To my relief, I saw an incoming call from Mark

After telling him how I mistook the simple moonlight reflection of a tree for an intruder, Mark reminded me, "Hey, we aren't in Johannesburg. It's far, far safer here."

He was right, and his reassuringly steady voice calmed me down considerably. I finally managed to doze off, tossing and turning restlessly.

I didn't feel much better in the morning. Waking up on my own, the harsh reality of the deadly Ebola epidemic and what we were up against in trying to get Missy out of the country hit me like a juggernaut.

I was in a bad way, exhausted and overwhelmed by the worry of whether we would find somewhere to stay on Friday when we had to leave the Ecolodge.

Mark phoned to see if I was all right and said he would come over to be with me that night. That was just the tonic I needed. It was as though a boulder had been lifted off my shoulders.

I spent most of the day on the patio outside the room with Missy, venturing out only for a short walk in the midafternoon.

Missy had great fun, climbing on the chairs and the balcony balustrade. Some staff members walked past and many stopped to chat to me. Most knew about the Ebola outbreak, although amazingly, considering the non-stop news coverage, a few had no idea. I used the opportunity to tell them how hunting wild animals was a massive Ebola risk, and they should tell their friends and families not to do it.

In turn they shared their stories with me. I was stunned at how many Liberians knew of various chimpanzees being kept as pets.

One that still sticks in my mind was a man telling me that he had a friend who had trained his pet chimpanzee to fetch and carry stuff for him like a lackey. This was not hard to imagine as chimps are remarkably intelligent creatures.

Even more distressing, other staff members told me about chimps being kept in a cage at a nightclub in

Monrovia's Congo Town for the amusement of revelers, who gave them alcohol.

There was no shortage of horror stories of what was happening to these endangered animals in captivity. For most modern-day chimps there is no respite. In the forests they are hunted for bushmeat; in the towns they are tormented and abused.

That, I vowed, was not going to happen to Missy.

As the day wore on, I could hardly wait for Mark to arrive. When he did, it seemed all my troubles were far away. That night sleep came easily.

Mark had another early start the next day. As soon as he left I started to feel vulnerable again. I really needed to think positively, as Mark was doing. The key issue was that we had to find a place for Missy this weekend. I started dialing around.

No luck. Each phone call resulted in the same answers. Either a straight no, from people who couldn't care less, or else an apologetic refusal, from those with a conscience but unable to do anything.

A typical answer was from a friend called Blake, an expat managing a lodge close to town. I knew it was a long shot, but phoned anyway and asked him if I could sneak Missy into one of the rooms.

Blake was from Kenya and wanted to get involved with helping animals in West Africa. But his hands were tied as the lodge owner said pointblank that it was too 'dangerous' to have a chimp on the premises.

Blake, knowing the facts about the Ebola virus, gave a heartfelt apology.

"If it was my lodge I would take you and Missy in. I wish I could help. But I can't take that chance."

I had no idea what to do next.

Twenty-two

THAT NIGHT I WAS ON MY own again at the Libassa Ecolodge. As much as I wished Mark could be with me, I knew that he was also drained from the last few days.

Missy's accommodation problems were wearing him down, but he never complained.

Also, although the golf course was now open, he personally needed to supervise the maintenance and check that the greens were being properly watered. This meant he had to be there first thing in the morning each day.

Thursday arrived. I now had only one day to find somewhere to stay for the weekend.

Instead, more bad news was to follow. Mark phoned Phillip about the worsening situation at our end and to see if the process could be speeded up.

Instead we got another bombshell. The worst news possible.

The South African government had put a stop to all wild animals entering the country from West Africa.

Ebola had finally shut us down completely.

I was stunned. I could barely take in what he had just said. My resilience crumbled.

I phoned my sister Sandra in Johannesburg. Bitterness consumed every fiber of my body. It seemed that everything was conspiring against us. From Missy being kicked out of the compound, to the two of us being virtually on the run trying to find somewhere to stay, to being told that Chimp Eden, our happy ending for Missy, had now been slammed shut in our face.

All the plans I had for Missy to have a safe, secure and loving home went up in smoke.

Sandra shared the news with our cousin Robyn Kapral, who had 'met' Missy with me on a few Skype chats. Robyn decided she also wanted to help.

"Have you tried the hotels? Surely there is someone who lives in Liberia who will let you stay at their house?"

Sandra and Robyn were doing their best to be supportive, but with the current emergency and sheer exhaustion from all the anxiety, my tolerance levels were zero.

"There is no one we know who will let us stay with them," I snapped. "I have also tried every compound I know of, and a hotel will be an absolute no-go with all the other guests."

I immediately bit my tongue. Every kind effort they made to help us resulted in me jumping down their throats. I wasn't in a good place at all.

Mark, who was at the farm, promised to get to the lodge as soon as he could.

When he arrived, he took one look at me and realized that I was actually in worse shape than he first thought. With all the stress, I hadn't eaten much or slept well.

I looked exactly how I felt; a wreck.

Phillip had told Mark that the ban of animals coming from Ebola-stricken West Africa would be in force for at least four months, possibly much longer. But no one knew exactly how long. Only once Liberia was deemed Ebola free, followed by a quarantine period to ensure it was no longer a threat, would animals from West Africa again be admitted into South Africa. This could take up to a year, for all we knew. And we would be leaving Liberia within weeks.

Mark decided that for my own good I needed to take a break. He suggested we take Missy to the farm to live with Adele for a few days.

I was outraged. "How can you even suggest that?"

"We have run out of options, Crocodile."

"I refuse! I can't leave her with Adele. I will not allow her to be left in a cage or tied to a tree. I can't be so far away from her knowing she might be starving or sick. She needs constant attention, as a baby chimp is with its mother all of the time.

"In fact," I continued, "she would be better off with her mother in Heaven than going back to the farm."

I stopped, stunned at what I had just said. Had we actually got to that? Was this the proverbial elephant in the room that could no longer be ignored?

Would I really consider having Missy euthanized?

The next instant I crashed headfirst onto the wooden floor, Missy still clutching my side. I was having a severe panic attack.

I tried to get up, but my legs were like jelly. My whole body felt weak and wobbly.

Fortunately, Missy was fine, although she must have got quite a shock when I suddenly collapsed, taking her down like a ton of bricks with me.

That night I cracked. I couldn't even be strong for Missy. I wept uncontrollably until dawn broke.

The next day we had to leave the Libassa Ecolodge as the weekend started and guests would soon arrive. We still had nowhere else to go. Things were not good.

I looked at Missy, clinging to my hip. I then felt my strength returning. I had pledged to see this though. Nothing was going to stop me. Just as Mark was being strong for me, I was going to be strong for Missy. The Ebola travel ban on West African animals may have been the final straw. But looking into Missy's trusting eyes, I vowed I would fight this to the end.

The fightback started on several fronts. Back in South Africa Robyn created a Facebook page pleading for someone to take us in. Friends who knew our situation started phoning other sanctuaries around the world.

We soon learnt that it was not only South Africa refusing to take in chimpanzees with the current Ebola hysteria. There was now a global ban on all primates from West Africa.

I also discovered that although there are quite a lot of international chimpanzee sanctuaries, most are at full capacity. That alone shows the dire straits these beautiful creatures are in.

Chimps sanctuaries specialize in caring for rescued animals which have either been orphaned, illegally kept as pets or confiscated from ruthless smugglers. Like Chimp Eden, they are excellent last resorts of refuge, and the animals admitted are the lucky ones.

For most others, the situation – as we were finding with Missy – is dire. Thousands of baby chimps captured in the wild either starve to death or die from broken hearts when wrenched from their families. Many perish after being wounded when bushmeat hunters kill their mothers.

Those that survive and aren't illegally smuggled to other countries often spend their entire lives tied to a pole with little or no shelter from the blazing heat and pelting rain. Most are fed the wrong diet, while many are hardly fed at all. Chimpanzees kept outside nightclubs – as staff at the Ecolodge told me – are there purely as an 'attraction' for clients and regularly plied with booze and fizzy drinks.

Not all sanctuaries are for wild chimps. In America there are 'retired' chimps that have been used in the movie and entertainment industry, or for medical research. Most are in a terrible condition now that their 'services' are no longer required. These poor animals' only hope for a better life is in an urban sanctuary, where they spend their final years.

Nature is cruel. But no creature torments fellow travelers on this planet as much as we humans do.

A hunter selling a chimp in Monrovia

Missy learning to be a chimp at the CCC

Her name is Missy

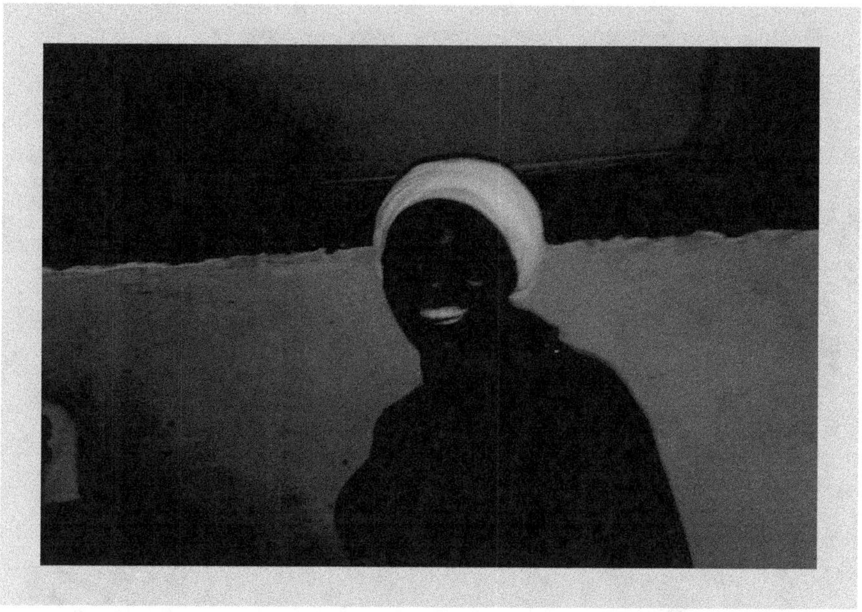

Etag and Michael Jedig Jensen – good friends to both Missy and us

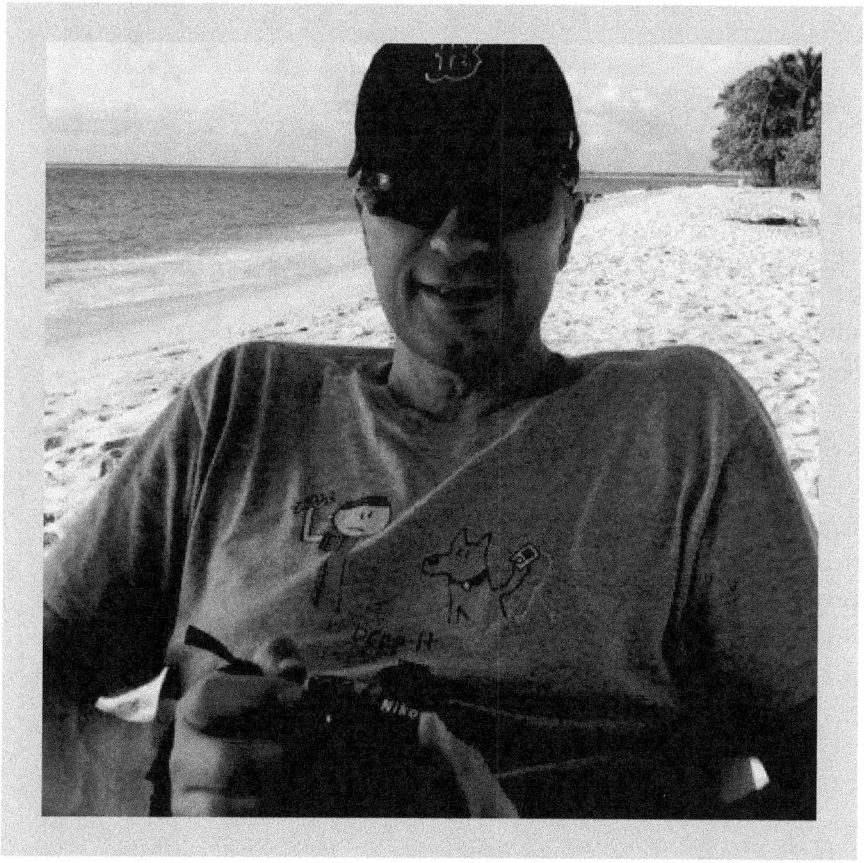

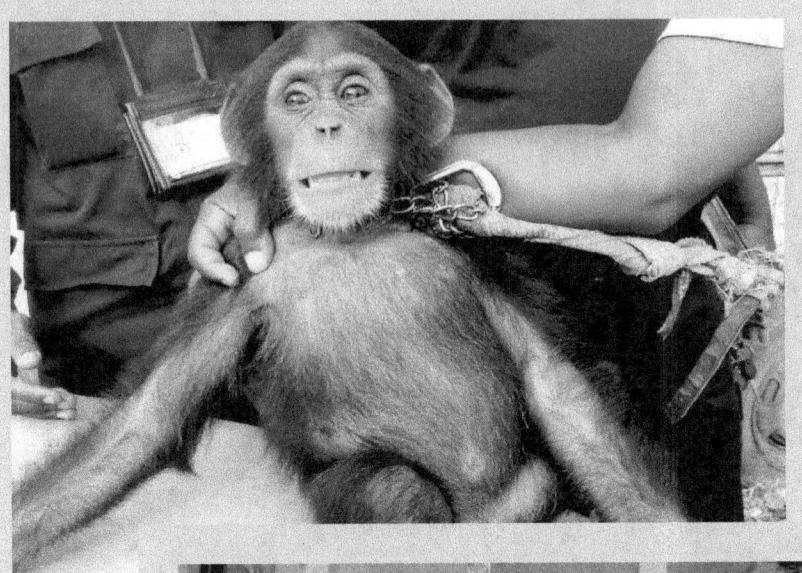

The reality facing many chimps in West Africa. Sweetpea (bottom) was rescued from this living hell

170

Twenty-three

FRIDAY MORNING WAS ANOTHER EARLY START for us as we left the Ecolodge. Rudolph generously only charged us half price rates, but even so it was a costly few days for us.

Missy and I went with Mark to the farm. I had previously refused outright when Mark suggested that we leave Missy with Adele for a few days. But I now realized we had no other option, so I reluctantly agreed.

"But only for the weekend!" I stressed.

Mark nodded.

We arrived at the gate and Peter stopped at the security hut. Adele was there and we asked if she could look after Missy for a couple of days.

She shook her head. "I can't tak Missy home. The commu'ty be too 'fraid."

We hadn't bargained for that. Adele may have been a last resort, but we never thought she would actually refuse.

There was nothing to do but to drive off.

I was now starting to stress again. Mark, for the first time, also looked as if he'd received a body blow. The enormous worry was now taking its toll on him as well. He had been so calm and so strong for both me and Missy for so long.

Neither of us were sure what the next step was, and for the first time we found ourselves snapping at each other.

I was worried about Missy, but Mark was also extremely worried about me. He saw firsthand that I had not coped well on my own at the Libassa Ecolodge. He didn't want me to be too far away from him again for my own good. We needed to stay together.

But at that minute it was not even a question of staying together – for the simple reason that we had nowhere to stay if we wanted to keep Missy with us. This was what I had been agonizing about all week. I had no idea what to do.

Then out of the blue, Phoebe called.

"I have a place for you and Missy," she said.

I was stunned. A scrap of good news at last.

"It's my friend Juliet's apartment," Phoebe continued. "The NGO that she works for has rented it for the year, but it has no running water at the moment. So she's moved in with me. It'll be fine for you and Missy in the meantime."

"I cannot tell you what this means to us," I said.

"Bring Missy over for a visit, then we'll take you to the apartment. It is in Sinkor, just down the road."

"You are the best Phoebe, see you later." I replied, relief washing over me like a balm.

This was a huge weight off our shoulders. However, Mark, seeing how strung out we both were, insisted that we stay together at our apartment at Ocean View that night.

"The letter they sent about Missy asked if we can find another place as soon as possible. That's what we are doing – finding her another place. And we are doing our best to make it as soon as possible."

He rubbed his eyes, obviously as exhausted as I was.

"But I don't actually care right now, Crocodile. Tonight you and Missy are staying at the compound."

This was not open for discussion. When Mark makes up his mind, it stays made. Instinctively I knew that he was right.

After such a week of worry, we all needed to be together in familiar surroundings.

Twenty-four

JUST BEFORE WE ARRIVED AT Ocean View, I put Missy on my lap and draped a towel over her to hide her from prying eyes.

Peter then nonchalantly drove past security at the gate and parked the car right next to our apartment door. It was only a few yards, but it was crucial that Missy was not seen.

I grabbed a couple of bags to hide her, and as swiftly as I could, snuck into the apartment and went straight to the bathroom off our bedroom.

Mark and Peter brought the remaining bags inside. What a relief! We had managed to get Missy inside without being spotted. Or so we hoped.

I was looking forward to a hot, proper shower. At that stage it seemed to me to be an almost unimaginable luxury.

"What if someone comes to see us, Foxy?"

Mark shrugged. "Let's worry about that if it happens."

"I don't want anyone to know that Missy is here and I'm not in the mood for visitors. If anyone comes, I'm staying in the bedroom. Just tell them that I'm not well and need to be alone."

To keep Missy amused, I went to the pile of things we had brought from the car to look for Mogli. After a fruitless search, I asked Mark to double-check the car trunk.

He looked all over without any luck. Then I realized I must have left the toy chimp at the Libassa Ecolodge, probably stuck between the wall and the bed as that was where Missy kept throwing it.

This was a problem as Missy would start getting restless soon if her beloved 'friend' was not around.

I quickly phoned Rudolph to ask the lodge staff to fetch Mogli and I would get Peter to collect the toy the next day.

As soon as I hung up, Phoebe phoned to ask us to come and see Juliet's apartment where we would be staying.

Once again, we had to sneak out of the compound. Peter checked that the coast was clear and then opened the car door so I could rush straight for the backseat. I leaned forward with her, pretending I had dropped something on the floor and hoping the dark seats would provide camouflage as we drove out onto the road.

Phoebe lived in a spacious, two-bedroom apartment in a well-maintained and popular compound. We arrived and Missy, who sensed that Phoebe adored her, gave her and Juliet a warm welcome.

She then voluntarily left my side and climbed onto Phoebe's lap. I could hardly believe my eyes. This had never happened before. Missy had never gone to anyone else without being physically handed over. And that was usually accompanied by some anguished yelps.

They had a great time playing together and it was a breakthrough seeing Missy now becoming braver and more trusting. I was so impressed that I decided I would sneak into the next room to meet Frankie, an orphaned potto that Phoebe had recently rescued.

Frankie was blind in one eye, the result of a nasty injury received when his mother was killed for bushmeat. I had never heard of pottos before and was keen to see a live one. It's a small, tropical, tree-dwelling, nocturnal African primate, that looks like a bushbaby

That was not a good idea. When Missy saw that I had gone she became frantic trying to find me. To calm her, Phoebe picked her up, and as a result, Missy nipped her.

I quickly went to fetch her and placed her between myself and Phoebe. The nip had not been serious, and Phoebe, who truly understands animals, knew it was not malicious. Missy had just panicked when I left, despite the fact that she was very comfortable with Phoebe.

Telling us about our new temporary 'home', Juliet said that for several weeks now they'd had no running water whatsoever. The owner had not even had the courtesy to respond to her frequent requests to sort it out. Despairing that the problem would ever be fixed, she decided she had had enough and moved in with Phoebe.

Eager to see our new digs and not wanting to overstay our welcome, we got up to go.

Phoebe and Juliet suggested that with the Ebola panic, it would be best not to let anyone, apart from Cooper the caretaker, see Missy when we arrived. She gave us the keys as well as Cooper's cell phone number.

The apartment was behind a beauty shop in an old concrete building, not far from our compound on the main road. Juliet had already told Cooper about us and he was at the gate to let us in.

Once again, I bundled Missy up in a towel. I was not going to take any chances, even though there did not seem to be anyone around. Without being asked, Peter also parked the car at an angle to restrict the line of sight of anyone watching. He was now so used to the cloak and daggers game that we were forced to play wherever we went anywhere with Missy.

The apartment was a bit of a disappointment as it was small, just a bedroom with an *en suite* bathroom and a lounge. There was no kitchen.

The mattress on the bed was old and stained, the faded curtains were ragged, looking dull and dreary. All were in need of a good wash. Which was a problem, as there was no water available.

Cooper told us that all the other apartments were also empty. Most of the previous tenants had, like Juliet, left because they were unhappy about not having running water. Two, however, had left the country altogether because of Ebola.

This was good news for us. With nobody else in the compound, there would be no complaints about Missy.

When we returned to Ocean View it was dark and so we managed to sneak her into our apartment again – hopefully – unnoticed. At last I could take the much-needed warm shower that I had promised myself.

Exhausted by the events of the past two weeks I went to bed early and fell into a dead sleep.

When Annie arrived for work the next morning, I begged her please not to tell anyone that Missy had spent the night with us.

She nodded. She was one of the few people who understood that Missy was not the problem.

Ignorance was.

Twenty-five

I HAD HEARD ABOUT AN Ethiopian Veterinary Surgeon called Etag. Her full name is Etagegnehu D Belayneh, but most people in Liberia couldn't remember or pronounce that so they called her Etag.

Etag had a small veterinary practice in town, and Mark and I thought it would be a good idea to go and have a chat with her about Missy's situation. Maybe she had some contacts or ideas about what we could do.

Her practice was quite close to the compound, and Peter parked on the road near the entrance. I got out and while walking to towards the office with Missy on my hip, an elderly Liberian man saw us and started shouting.

"Yo' brin' Ebol' to our coun'ry! Yo' killin' our peepl!"

I said nothing and kept walking. Which was probably a good thing as I could feel my anger rising.

Moments later a few more people gathered and joined in the increasingly aggressive tirade against us and the 'buboon'.

This time it was Mark, not me, who responded. He was not intimidated at all by their growing belligerence. Mark is not someone you threaten.

"We would not have this chimp if your people didn't kill her mother," he snapped back at them. "And she is a chimp, NOT a baboon! You go and tell the bushmeat hunters, not us, that they are the ones bringing Ebola to your people!"

The crowd got larger and larger, shouting, swearing and pointing fingers at Missy and me. As the uproar intensified, so did the anger and hatred. One person was making throat-slitting gestures.

Thoroughly alarmed, I managed to slip into the vet's office with Missy, leaving the baying mob outside.

The building was a small narrow room with a counter on each side displaying various veterinary medicines and supplies. Most of the stuff was animal feed, some dog and cat food, and a small display of pet apparel.

Etag was consulting with a customer in a room at the far end of the shop. There was no air conditioner or fan, and after a couple of minutes I was dripping with sweat.

Etag had two staff members, who – like most Liberians – were friendly and kind. They asked me many questions about Missy and were genuinely concerned about her welfare. Then the door opened and Etag walked out followed by her client and their pet dog.

Mark and I introduced ourselves. Etag was a beautiful, exotic woman with a classically sculptured face and radiated serenity. She was a little older than I imagined, probably in her late 30s, and I could see right away that she was a calm and caring soul. She returned the greeting and introduced herself as Etag, not as Dr Belayneh, a testament to her humble nature.

She asked us how old Missy was, and when she mentioned how obviously attached Missy was to me, I couldn't hold back the tears. Mark told her our dilemma; the almost impossible task of trying to get Missy into a sanctuary, and the looming deadline as we were leaving the country in a couple of weeks' time.

Etag listened carefully. She was well aware of the dreadful situation facing chimpanzees with the Ebola epidemic, and said she knew of some people who may be willing to help us. She said she would contact them and get back to me as soon as she could.

That was heartening news. But what was even more fantastic was that she also offered to put me and Missy up at her home.

We thanked her and left the building, bracing ourselves for more abuse from hostile people in the street. Luckily, the bellicose crowd had dispersed, although the old man who had started the nonsense was still there. He rushed up and continued shouting insults as we climbed into the car. We ignored him.

Peter sped off. I think he was as spooked by the aggression as we were. Liberians are a friendly nation, but in times of dread and uncertainty, they can be roused to a mob frenzy. And Ebola was a horror show now embedded in the national psyche.

That's why, despite my anger at the abuse we were subjected to, I could to a certain extent understand the hysteria.

The epidemic was peaking at that stage and if anyone in Liberia became ill, the immediate fear was being diagnosed with Ebola.

The terror of being dispatched to the Ebola treatment center, where an Ebola patient would not have any further contact with their loved ones and possibly die a terrible death, often prevented people with any illness from going for medical care.

Even telling someone you were not feeling well was a risk. Understandably, many sick people simply kept quiet pretending they were healthy. A sometimes fatal spin-off of this was that other illnesses such as malaria, which can be just as deadly, also went undetected.

Eventually, the sick person would be too far gone to respond to treatment that would earlier have saved their lives.

There were also rumors that some medical staff refused to go near or treat anyone with symptoms related to Ebola.

But seeing such street anger up close and in our faces as we had experienced outside Etag's office made it abundantly clear that we now would have to hide Missy wherever we took her.

Her life was in danger; that much was certain.

Twenty-six

THE U.N. RELEASED A DETAILED, easy-to-read statement explaining the realities and myths of Ebola to try and lessen the panic gripping much of West Africa, which many compound owners and businesses printed off for their staff to read.

I got copies as well and showed it to everyone I could. It proved that as far as an Ebola-free animal was concerned, Missy ticked all the boxes. While this did not convince all, at least Annie and Peter now knew with absolute certainty that Missy was not a risk.

Otherwise, for us the days of fear and uncertainty continued. Mark, as always, started his day by driving to the farm to check up on the golf course, and as it was somewhere where Missy could at least enjoy fresh air and be outdoors, we often went with.

For Missy, even a car ride was an adventure. She spent the journey clambering from the backseat to the front to sit with Mark, then climbing back to be me, then along the top of the rear seat, peering out of the back window.

Another trick was clutching the steel bars of the headrest with one hand, swinging back and forth with a happy expression just as she used to do on her improvised 'gyms' in our apartment.

While Mark checked the course, Missy and I played in the fields close by. The extreme heat was something I still couldn't get used to. There were plenty of shady trees for her to climb, although she would only climb within my reach. If we weren't near a tree, Missy would hold my hand and run on two legs on the grass, just like a human toddler.

When that grew tiring, I would grab both her hands and swing her like a merry-go-round. Once that stopped, she would take my hand and do a little jive, demanding another swing. Then another. And another. It didn't take long for me to be sweating like a marathon runner.

On one occasion Mark finished what needed to be done before lunch and said, "Why don't we visit Edwin?"

Edwin was a friend who lived on the far side of the golf course. We had first met him at a social function on the farm with Jack and Dorothy and he had invited us on a couple of previous occasions to pop in for a visit. This time we decided to take him up on it.

Hoping that Missy wouldn't be a problem for Edwin, we drove down to his house. He was very pleased to see us, including Missy.

He was a fascinating man and a great raconteur. I loved listening to the stories of his interesting life.

But while Edwin was regaling us with his adventures, Mark suddenly got a call. I could see by the frown on his face that, once again, this was not good news.

It was Danny, the manager at Ocean View. Unfortunately, someone had seen us sneaking Missy into our apartment the night before, despite our elaborate precautions.

Danny was extremely agitated and rude towards Mark. He had every right to be upset as we had been told that Missy was no longer welcome, but even so, his attitude was a little too belligerent.

Mark handled the volatile situation perfectly, saying it would not happen again. We had another place for Missy, he assured the compound manager.

We refused to let Danny's aggressive attitude spoil a wonderful afternoon with Edwin, who like so many other people, was totally blown away by Missy's similarity to a human baby.

As soon as we left, I phoned Etag, the vet, to see if she had any positive news. Unfortunately, not. She said she had phoned two of her clients whom she thought might be able to help, but had no luck with either.

So we were back to square one.

Etag then invited Missy and I to stay at her house that evening. As there was no still water or electricity at Juliet's apartment, I gladly accepted her offer.

I went to our compound to have a shower and to pack a few things. Etag offered to fetch us when she had finished work, and her driver, Jack, phoned for directions.

As soon as I heard the car arrive, I asked Mark to help me carry my bags and Missy's cot with her milk and food.

This time I didn't try to hide Missy. I didn't care if any of the snooping expats or security guards saw us.

I had had enough.

Libassa Ecolodge and (below) rainy season in Monrovia

Guey, tethered to an old car and (below) the rainforest

Missy and her friend Labe at the CCC (top) and (below) a content
and healthy Missy

Twenty-seven

ETAG LIVED IN CONGO TOWN, a sprawling suburb in the south of the city. Unlike Mark, I was unfamiliar with Monrovia's districts besides the supermarkets or shops that were predominantly on the main road.

So I had never been to Congo Town before, and unfortunately for my nerves on those helter-skelter roads, Jack was not a cautious chauffeur like Peter. He drove like most Liberians, squeezing into impossibly small gaps and hooting loudly to claim right of way.

I tried to concentrate on where we were going in case I got lost and had to find my way home. But as so many roads looked identical with rows of dilapidated buildings and the constant hustle and bustle of people milling about, it was impossible.

Just before we reached Etag's house, Mark phoned to see if I was okay.

"I wasn't happy with you going off to Etag's house on your own. Phone me as soon as you arrive."

Mark is a big fan of gadgets and had both our iPhones linked to an app that shows our locations. He tracked the entire drive through the city to Etag's house to make sure he knew exactly where I was.

Etag's home nestled among a cluster of other houses. Most were decent-sized buildings, albeit all pretty old, but there were also a fair number of huts and small square concrete structures.

Etag's house had high walls with barbed wire jutting from the top, giving a lot of privacy, while the front gate was secured with a thick chain and lock.

She took me to the room that Missy and I were to spend the night. To my surprise, it actually was her bedroom. She said she would sleep in the guest room. I protested, not wanting her to give up her own space, but she insisted. I must have looked embarrassed at her fantastic hospitality, but she said that having a guest was a privilege in her culture.

Even though Etag was a highly-educated and successful woman, her home was equipped with just the bare basics. This was no fancy expat house by any means. In fact, the house didn't even have running water, so we used a five-liter container in the bathroom.

There was also no power, so Etag gave me a flashlight to see in the dark.

A little later, one of Etag's friends came to visit and we went outside to chat.

Missy sat with me on a bench, but behind us was a window with burglar bars. This was too much for her. To her, burglar guards were not there to deter criminals; they were for climbing! Within a second or two, she was swinging along as happily as Tarzan. Or Jane, in her case.

Unfortunately, this didn't go down too well with Etag's friend who shrieked when Missy started swinging towards her. I had to remind myself that with Ebola paranoia many people were terrified of having any jungle animal anywhere near them.

I apologized and called Missy back to me. We then sat further away so as not to disturb anyone.

This was a timely reminder of how careful I had to be with Missy when other people were around. It also showed how far Etag was prepared to go in helping Missy and me – even showing her friends that we were welcome in her house.

When the woman left, Etag and I talked about life in our home countries. But the conversation soon returned to what was uppermost in both our minds; Missy's future.

I said my biggest fear was that Missy would not have any proper care when Mark and I left. It wasn't just the constant love and attention that she needed, I was equally concerned that she wouldn't get enough milk and proper nutrition.

Etag knew exactly what I was talking about, and suggested that perhaps we could teach someone how to care for her until a decent sanctuary was found. In the interim, she said, Missy could stay at her home.

I loved that idea.

While we were happily chatting away, Mark was obviously still worried about me. Every now and again I had to stop talking to Etag to answer a barrage of texts.

First: "Do you want me to fetch you?"

Then: "Are you okay?"

Followed by: "I am not happy that you are in a place with no air con. If you get malaria you won't be any good for Missy!"

I tried to put his mind at rest: "Foxy, I am really fine. I have mosquito spray. Etag is such a divine person and wonderful host."

However, with all the texting my cell phone's battery started to run low. This could be a problem if Peter couldn't find Etag's house the next morning as I would have no way to contact him.

Fortunately, he did find us, arriving early and as we had nowhere else to go, we once again drove to the farm.

The baboon that was usually tethered to a tree near the entrance was nowhere to be seen when we arrived. I thought it had been moved somewhere else because of the

Ebola scare, but that wasn't the case. Instead, the security guard said that one of the farm workers had stabbed it. The knife-wound was not fatal and the animal was recovering somewhere else on the farm.

I never found out why the defenseless, tied-up baboon had been stabbed. Even with the Ebola hysteria stalking the country like a horseman of the Apocalypse, who would want to do something like that?

We were indeed living in strange times.

Twenty-eight

THAT EVENING WE SNEAKED Missy into the apartment again. To hell with the prying and ignorant tenants who had previously informed on us.

To hell with the manager who had shouted at us.

Each day, the search to find a sanctuary continued. With the help of my sister Sandra and cousin Robyn, as well as many other friends and family, word was now getting around fast.

I think by now almost every chimp sanctuary in the world knew about Missy and was being bombarded with emails. Many of these were sent without Mark and I even knowing, such was the fantastic support we had from people who cared.

But the situation on the ground was still dire. The date for our imminent departure from Liberia was drawing close and we were rapidly running out of time as well as options.

The constant need to hide Missy was also taking its toll and stress and fatigue gnawed at my shattered nerves. Annie was now getting worried about me.

"Gaal, yo' can't worr' 'bout dis too much. Look how much yo' hav' reduced!"

By reduced, she meant how much weight I had lost in just a couple of weeks. She was absolutely right. I physically resembled the wreck I was emotionally.

I also by now couldn't face going to the farm again and asked Mark if Peter could drop me off at the Sinkor Road apartment that Phoebe's friend Juliet had lent us.

I called the caretaker Cooper to let him know I would be arriving and packed food, water and a bag with Missy's toys. Annie went outside to see if the coast was clear while Peter started the car.

As always, I was hugely relieved when we got through the compound gate without Missy being seen. Although we were never a hundred per cent sure if that was the case. The last time we only found out that she had been spotted after the irate call from Danny the manager.

Cooper was waiting at the gate and Peter parked at an angle so no one could see me climbing out with Missy. As usual, I covered her with a towel.

It was stifling hot and Mark and Peter tried to get the generator working without any success. The bathroom had no water, so obviously Juliet's regular complaints to management were still being ignored.

197

The-entrance consisted of a wooden door and a solid steel security gate, which Mark told me to lock when he left, as well as all the windows. He was worried about the security of the compound and must have had a sixth sense that something could happen.

Within a few minutes I felt as though I was steaming in a sauna. The heat and claustrophobia was overwhelming. Fortunately, I had brought along a lot of water otherwise I would have soon dehydrated.

Missy didn't seem to notice the heat at all, playing happily with the toys I had brought along. To her, this was just another one of many adventures. Everything was new and exciting.

We still had not found Mogli, but the large plastic container for Missy's toys was perfect for her to romp around in. I put a pillow at the bottom to cushion the hard base, and Missy would dive in, climb out, and then dive back in again, sometimes doing an acrobatic head-over-heels in the process.

When she eventually got tired of that particular game, she decided to read a magazine with me, mimicking my moves. But instead of turning the pages, she figured it was far more fun just to tear them out. In no time the apartment looked like a shredding machine.

The morning dragged, but despite the heat, I managed to nod off while Missy had a nap.

At about lunchtime, Mark texted me to say that he had finished at the farm and would see me soon.

I was drenched in sweat from the heat of the locked apartment and my hair hung in limp damp locks. Reckoning Mark would be back soon, I decided to try and cool down a little and, ignoring his instructions, unlatched the door and gate.

I picked Missy up and we sat on the threshold together, reveling in the fresh air. Nobody could see us from the road.

Or so I thought. Suddenly a figure loomed out of nowhere. A Liberian man was standing right in front of me. One moment there was nothing, then suddenly a strange rather sinister looking person was just a meter away.

My initial panic was that he had seen Missy and I tried to cover her. The scream died in my throat as he said he wanted money

I told him I didn't have money on me. I was amazed at how calm my voice sounded. I knew I had to protect Missy at all costs.

He scowled at me for a moment. Then still staring hard into my face he said he didn't believe me. I must have some money.

I quickly weighed up my options. There were none. He was too close. I didn't have the vital seconds necessary to jump back into the apartment and slam the door. He would be onto me too quickly.

Things didn't look good.

Then, with extreme good fortune, Cooper suddenly appeared.

The man turned and ran off.

Cooper had certainly saved the day. He stayed with me until Mark arrived. We talked about his life, his dream of becoming a computer programmer and of course the animals in Liberia. I pointed to Missy and tried to convince him that the bushmeat trade would kill off all animals in the jungle like her and he nodded. He asked many questions and seemed very eager to learn more, I believe I had success in just the short time we sat chatting. He seemed inspired to spread the word.

I couldn't expect Mark to stay with me at the apartment with no lights and water. He instead suggested I phone Betty at the Ocean View compound and ask her if she would stay with Missy that night.

Bettie had looked after Missy the second time Mark and I went back to South Africa, and they had bonded nicely. That seemed a good idea, so I called her.

"I don' think Fadi (her boss) or my com'unty wan' me to look aft' Missy no mor'," was Bettie's reply.

What a letdown. Mark then said he would go to our compound and ask Annie.

Annie was also a little dubious at first so Mark made her a substantial cash offer. She said she first needed to go home to discuss it with her sister, who would have to look after Annie's children in her absence.

Annie later phoned to give us the thumbs up and she would be at the apartment in an hour.

What a relief.

I waited at the apartment with Missy while Mark and Peter went to the supermarket to get a five-liter drum of water and food for Annie.

The electricity was now working but Cooper told us it was extremely unreliable and we would need the generator as back-up. Mark gave Cooper money for diesel and we also bought Annie cellphone airtime so she could call if she needed anything.

It was late afternoon when I handed Missy over to Annie. As usual, Missy started performing and it broke my heart. But I knew she would settle down after a while.

It was instant luxury walking into our apartment. The air conditioner blasting gloriously cool air was absolutely heavenly after what felt like an entire day in a Turkish bath.

It was the first time in weeks that I did not have Missy with me. With a shock, I suddenly realized how much I missed her. I was not prepared for the sudden wrench.

She had totally stolen my heart.

Twenty-nine

A LITTLE LATER MARK AND I went for a walk down to the swimming pool. I needed the fresh air and we both needed quality time together.

For the past week, virtually every minute of the day had either been spent making plans for Missy or hiding her from snooping eyes. When we weren't discussing Missy, we were thinking about what to do about her.

Then as we were getting ready for dinner, Annie called. She was not happy. The electricity had gone off, which was not a surprise, but the generator had now also broken down. The result was a complete power blackout. She was sitting in total darkness apart from the light from her cellphone.

I told her we would bring some emergency equipment over right away and grabbed two flashlights, candles and matches.

When we arrived, the doors were open and Annie was sitting on the couch fanning herself with what was left of my magazine.

Missy was on the couch next to her. When she saw me she cried to be picked up.

Annie was clearly miserable. "I can't stay her' in dis apar'men'. It i' too hot!"

Mark look at the generator. It had a broken alternator, which Cooper obviously had been unable to fix. So there was no chance of getting it going for the night.

I was now agitated and told Annie that she could go home and I would stay with Missy. Despite the heat, which was so intense it was almost unbearable, I was happy to do so.

But Mark strenuously disagreed and told Annie that he would get the generator fixed first thing the next day. She only would have to endure one hot, uncomfortable night.

I had no energy to argue, so I let Annie decide.

She nodded. "Okay. I sta'." But added that she didn't think anyone would be able to tolerate such a 'furnace' for too long.

I gave Annie the flashlights and candles, telling her with my usual obsessiveness only to have candles alight while she was awake and to watch that Missy didn't burn her fingers trying to play with them.

Handing Missy over to Annie for a second time was even more distressing.

The following morning, I woke early. I couldn't wait to be with Missy.

When I arrived at the apartment, Annie and Missy were sitting on the couch again, both looking a lot happier. The joy of seeing Missy and her reciprocal delight to see me also erased all my stresses from the previous night.

Annie told me that Missy fell asleep soon after we left last night, only waking up once to have some milk. The heat had not affected her at all.

Not wanting to complicate Annie's situation with other staff members at Ocean View, some of whom still thought Missy was an Ebola risk, Peter dropped her off around the corner and out of sight.

Peter and Mark then fetched me and Missy, and rather than endure another sweltering day at the apartment, I reluctantly went with Mark to the farm.

There were a lot of laborers, mostly women, working on the golf course. I kept some distance from them, but they always cheerfully greeted Missy. Not one complained or showed any concern about the baby chimp being around. That rather surprised me, seeing the often hostile reactions what we had got from other people in Monrovia.

Peter dropped Missy and I off at Juliet's apartment on the way back from the farm, and then went back to our compound to ask Annie if she would continue babysitting Missy for the rest of the week nights.

Annie, after the previous uncomfortable night with no power or running water, was obviously not keen. But with no one else willing, Mark made her another cash offer she could not refuse.

When she arrived, I let her know how grateful I was for her help. I knew it wasn't easy and told her that she was an absolute stalwart.

She smiled and said how much she appreciated the generous babysitting fees Mark was paying her. The money was going to help her and her family immensely.

She then again stressed how worried she was about me. I had lost far too much weight and the toll on my nerves was not sustainable.

I was touched by her obvious concern and said I hoped there would be a solution soon.

I then phoned Etag, our last remaining hope at the time. I was desperate to hear some good news – something we all needed. Something to hold onto.

Sadly, this was not to be. Etag told me she had contacted everyone she could think of. All had regretfully declined. She also added that no one was willing to baby sit Missy at her house.

Despite this, Missy had many fans doing what they could to help. A Danish expat friend, Michael Jedig Jensen, adored Missy and shared our sorrow and frustration for the many orphaned chimpanzees in the country. He wrote a beautiful story of Missy's short, traumatic life called 'When Ignorance kills the Innocent' which he posted on Facebook.

It was so poignant that I believed it pricked more than a few consciences.

We now had quite a following on social media and each day I got new Facebook messages and emails asking for news of Missy.

But even with all the tremendous support, even with all the information and facts about Ebola being given to locals and expats, we still didn't have anyone willing or able to look after her. It was a true Catch 22 situation with those who wanted to help being unable, and those able to help being unwilling.

After we left Missy and Annie, a couple of our expat friends at the compound came visiting. They all missed Missy, especially watching her climbing up and down the burglar bars each day.

This made me even angrier at the compound owners who had refused to change their minds, despite the fact that they clearly knew Missy was no threat.

In fact, the residents who had seemed most afraid of Missy, including the one whom we believed had reported us, by now had all left Liberia. So there was no reason for her still to be barred.

By turning their backs on a baby chimpanzee that, through no fault of her own was now literally on the run, many city people were showing that they were just as bad as the bushmeat hunters in the forests.

The flipside of the coin, however, was that with the growing awareness being generating on social media, the story of what Ebola ignorance was doing to wildlife was, in some microscopic way, being documented by what was happening to Missy. A small flame was still flickering.

While having dinner that night, we had the local radio station turned on. I listened stunned as the latest news bulletin instructed people to avoid chimpanzees and other primates at all costs, and then warned that 'only well-cooked bushmeat' should be eaten.

I could not believe it. In the beginning the radio stations had warned Liberians not to eat bushmeat at all. Now it had been downgraded to 'well cooked'.

"How can they encourage eating bushmeat with the Ebola epidemic in full swing?" I asked Mark, exasperated beyond belief.

It was a rhetorical question as the answer was self-explanatory. Utter madness.

At the very least, Ebola should have resulted in a total ban on killing *any* wild animal for consumption. It was too farfetched to believe that the authorities would sustain the ban once the Ebola epidemic passed, but at least it would have been a start.

I set my alarm extra early for the following morning, arriving at the apartment well in time for Annie to leave for her job at the compound.

She said she had had a better night than the previous one and would be prepared to babysit for the rest of the week.

At least one problem was solved.

Thirty

THE NEXT FEW DAYS PRETTY MUCH followed the same routine. I started to know what being on the run actually felt like.

I would wake early, impatient to get to Juliet's apartment to fetch Missy from Annie. Then we would go to the farm for some fresh air and exercise while Mark checked on the golf course. Sometimes we would stay there until lunch, other times until late into the afternoon.

In the evening, we would take Missy back to Juliet's apartment where she would spend the night with Annie. Each evening I would be torn apart and feel wretched at leaving Missy behind when we returned to Ocean View.

Like the proverbial Sword of Damocles hanging over us, the departure date for South Africa loomed closer and closer. We were now resigned to the fact that no sanctuary would accept Missy in the current climate of fear and loathing. But even worse, we had nowhere to place her temporarily to give us some breathing space to work things out until the Ebola crisis blew over.

209

So we grasped at whatever straws we could. One ray of light was when a friend in South Africa gave us a contact number for a veterinary surgeon in Zambia. We had nothing to lose, so without much hope, Mark contacted him.

It started off well. He said he had heard about Missy and decided to try and see if Zambia's state vet could make an exception in her case. He knew that Missy was definitely Ebola-free, and said he was determined to do whatever he could to help.

"Just give me a couple of days to sort some things out," were his parting words.

We hadn't had much positivity for weeks, and with the Zambian vet's determination, I allowed myself the luxury of being a tiny bit hopeful.

Mark thought that with the current unsatisfactory situation in having to drop Missy off at Juliet's apartment each night, it would be a good idea to ask Jack's wife Dorothy if she had a chalet available. There were several guest chalets on the farm, so it made perfect sense as Mark met Dorothy most days to discuss the golf course in any event.

Again we had no luck. Dorothy told us that a foreign company working on another project nearby had booked all the chalets for their employees for the next six months.

Mark then asked her if there was anyone at the farm who could take care of Missy for a short while after we left. He stressed that we would, obviously, continue trying to get Missy into a sanctuary, but we urgently needed someone to take care of her until the Ebola epidemic blew over. Dorothy knew that I would never give up fighting for Missy.

This was a pretty simple request. After all, Jack and Dorothy were the people who had first taken Missy in, buying her from the bushmeat hunter who killed her mother. They certainly owed Missy that.

But once again, it was not the answer we were hoping for. Dorothy agreed that Missy could stay at the farm, but she would have to be outside tied to a tree, like the poor baboon had been. I remembered the baboon well; it had been stabbed by a farm worker.

As diplomatically as I could (not very, according to Mark) I pointed out that it was unacceptable to tie a baby chimp to a tree, which prompted her condescending reply, "We have had many of them before and they were fine."

She then faced me and said, "How can you worry about an animal when people are dying from Ebola?"

I replied, "I prefer animals to people."

I now knew exactly where we stood. From that day on I did my best to avoid Dorothy.

However, Dorothy's answer posed a major question in my mind: What had happened to the 'many chimps they had before' that she spoke about? They certainly were no longer on the farm.

I decided it was probably a good thing that I did not know.

Thirty-one

HIDING MISSY FROM THE GENERAL PUBLIC during the Ebola nightmare, as well as from some of our less accommodating neighbors and the compound managers at Ocean View, was harrowing stuff.

We had a lot of narrow escapes.

But perhaps the scariest of all was a morning when Peter didn't arrive for work and Mark drove us to the farm.

At one of the chaotic four-way intersections that are a common feature on all Monrovia's streets, a traffic cop suddenly appeared in front of us, putting his hand out and indicating for Mark to stop.

After demanding to have a look at Mark's driver's license and car papers, he then inspected the vehicle from bonnet to boot. Finding everything in order, he poked his head through the window.

"Sir, r' yo' aware dat drivin' wid open shoe' again' de law in Liberiah?"

Mark shrugged. By now he was used to being stopped by certain policemen to get a quick shakedown for a bribe. Dishonest traffic cops deliberately target expats who were more likely to be unaware of the often arcane aspects of local law.

To be fair, it's not just expats. When Peter was driving we still got stopped, although nowhere near as often. The reason is obvious: expats usually have more money. And if they are not breaking the law, a misdemeanor is soon concocted. Mark reached for his wallet.

But when the cop told him the sum of the fine – five times the limit – we realized that this was no ordinary rip-off.

To get flagged down by a corrupt cop is never good, but this was particularly bad timing. It had been a massively stressful week, and when faced with the enormity of the bribe, normally calm Mark suddenly decided he had had enough. In spades.

"Get into the car," he said, his voice steady despite his anger. "We are going to the police station to sort this out. Now!"

Before I knew it, the cop was sitting in the back of the car, while I was in the front passenger seat with Missy sleeping on my lap under a towel.

If the cop saw her, Mark driving with 'open shoes' would be the least of our problems. Imagine the fine for having an 'Ebola threat', which we no doubt would have paid to save Missy's life.

Mark cleverly had recorded the conversation with the policeman on his phone. The cop suddenly realized this, and that the exorbitant fine – or rather, bribe – he was demanding was on record.

Suddenly this was a whole new ballgame and the cop started warily backing down. Mark said he would delete the incriminating evidence if the cop withdrew the fine, but the uniformed crook took some convincing that the recording was actually going to be erased.

While all this was happening, I was becoming more and more anxious that Missy would wake up and the cop would notice her. She was already starting to stir.

I had to get the cop to leave the car. And fast.

I nudged Mark and indicated that Missy would soon emerge with her usual happy face from under the towel. I begged him, speaking in Afrikaans, to end the argument and come to some agreement before Missy gave the game away with possible serious consequences.

Fortunately, in the nick of time Mark managed to convince the corrupt cop that the recording had in fact been deleted. Glaring daggers at us, he got out of the car.

Missy woke a few seconds later, full of beans and wanting to jump around. I was so relieved that I almost burst out laughing, despite the potentially precarious situation we had been in.

The weekend passed and early on Monday I took Missy to visit Etag at her practice. Luckily this time no one was hanging around outside to hurl abuse at us. In fact, there were now noticeably less people out on the streets as the Ebola stranglehold tightened.

Etag said she may have an update as she had heard of an expat who had a chimp as a pet, but had not manage to track her down yet. However, from what I gathered, it sounded as though it was the same expat I had bumped into at the supermarket some weeks ago who told me she also had not been able to get her animal into a sanctuary. I knew that was a dead-end as the woman said she and her husband were leaving Liberia soon.

Etag also had a contact number of a Liberian man who might be willing to look after Missy. This sounded more promising, so I immediately phoned him. He confirmed that he had kept a chimpanzee as a pet before. So he knew what he was in for. Or so he said.

"Where is your chimp?" I asked.

"She die' when she 'bout tree year' ol'. I wen' to de cage one mornin' and see she gon'."

That didn't sound good at all. Especially the word 'cage'.

"Missy is still a baby. I could never leave her in a cage," I told him. "She needs constant care.

"Also, she is not a pet. She is going to a chimpanzee sanctuary. As much as I appreciate your kind offer to look

215

after her, please understand that it is never okay to have a chimp as a pet. It is like caging a child."

I'm not sure if I convinced him. But it was another non-starter for us. Just one of many.

Then an expat sent me an email saying a Liberian who lived on a farm on the outskirts of Monrovia could help. I contacted him and he was agreeable. Only problem was that like the previous offer from the guy whose pet chimp had died on him, Missy would be kept in a cage.

Once again I declined. Missy needed constant love and attention. She was not going to get that care cramped up in a small cage.

Mark then managed to track down a South African who, we were told, had five chimps. However, he was no longer in the country and said he had left the chimps in the care of a Liberian farmer. He had given the farmer enough money to feed and care for the animals and would wire him more when funds ran low.

He then told Mark that he had also tried to send the chimps, which were now nearly fully grown, to various sanctuaries. But none had been able to take in five chimps in one go.

He said maybe the farmer would be able to take in Missy as well. He promised to get back to us with the Liberian man's number.

We didn't hear from him again.

By now Mark was working every contact he could. He again phoned the vet in Zambia who told him he was on his way to Lusaka to personally speak to the State Vet. He said the journey was a seven-hour drive, so he should have an answer for us the next day.

Then a lady from an animal organization phoned to tell me that as a last resort I could send Missy to a zoo in Abidjan, the capital of neighboring Cote d'Ivoire. The zoo had recently made a few improvements, but was still way below acceptable international standards.

There was only one lonely chimp at the zoo at the time. If we did choose to send Missy there it would be at our expense and she would never be able to leave.

That was a definite 'No.' Even though the zoo was trying to improve conditions for its animals, I was not willing for Missy to spend the rest of her life in a cage being gawked at by passing hordes.

Another problem with the Cote d'Ivoire was the ongoing internal strife. In the five-year civil war from 2002-7, I was told that most of the Abidjan Zoo's animals died after being abandoned and left to starve.

We had heard similar horror stories of the animals dying at the Monrovia Zoo during the war in Liberia. But in that case, instead of being left to starve, most of the animals were eaten.

Later, on the way home, we saw a chimp that didn't look much older than Missy on the road being dragged by a man with a chain. Mark and I were both shocked and appalled. Shocked because the man brazenly had a chimp in public with most people being so paranoid about Ebola, and appalled at the absolute and deliberate cruelty.

The next day Mark called the Zambian vet. I could tell from the way the conversation was going that it was yet another rejection in the growing list of rebuffs.

I took the phone from Mark and asked the vet what he would do in our situation. Mark no longer had a job so we had to leave Liberia. There was no one we could leave Missy with, and nowhere she could go.

So … what could we do?

His reply was gentle and sympathetic. "I would let her go and be with her mother. You have not failed her. You have done everything possible."

In other words, euthanasia.

I sobbed for hours. I needed to be alone to process the finality of that.

After a while, I pulled myself together. Collapsing in a heap was no good for anyone, let alone Missy.

But now that euthanasia was out in the open, part of me believed that she would be better with her mother in Heaven. What was the alternative? An uncertain future of loneliness, hunger, abuse and sorrow? Or even the risk of her being killed?

Many people shared our disappointment, but there were others who judged me harshly. Someone sent me an email saying that I had an illegal wild pet and I should immediately surrender Missy to the FDA.

Wow – if only I could! It would be the best thing in the world if the FDA had a safe sanctuary for her. But they didn't.

Then an organization sent me an email explaining the consequences of expats or Liberians buying chimps from hunters, as if I didn't already know only too well. Of course, I agreed with them; buying a chimp from a hunter does untold harm. Once he has pocketed the money, the hunter goes back to the forest to kill another family and capture another orphan to sell.

And so it goes on.

A manager at a sanctuary emailed me to say that I was as bad as the hunter. She suggested that I should start a sanctuary in Liberia for animals like Missy, even if meant leaving Mark. She told me her own amazing, heroic story of how she had started a sanctuary and what she had given up to do so. That really struck a chord with me. Despite her harsh words to me, I admired her. Although I would certainly not be leaving Mark!

Another person told me to smuggle Missy across the border. That too struck a chord.

Mark, my rock as always, saw that my conscience was getting the better of me.

"Crocodile, not everyone is made to be Mother Theresa, or rather Dian Fossey or Jane Goodall. You did more for Missy than most people would ever have done. Everyone who has judged you is quick to shoot their mouths off, but where are they? Why aren't they here to help you?"

That did calm me a little. I had to think rationally. If I was in my 20s, maybe I would have been braver. But now, in my mid 40s and without any financial backing, I had to be realistic.

Mark then remembered the manager at the Department of Agriculture saying that there was a place for orphaned chimps at a site where an American-biomedical laboratory was stationed. The person to speak to was Joseph Thomas, who had been working there for more than 30 years

By a stroke of good luck, Peter knew roughly where it was – somewhere near the airport, he said. Even though we were doubtful that the laboratory was still functioning or even there, we needed to explore every possibility.

Peter drove past the airport where the tar road abruptly ended and then we were bumping along a dirt track.

He stopped to ask a Liberian man if he knew how far we still had to go. The man told us to carry on for a little longer where we would see a signpost on the right.

A few more minutes down the rutted road and there it was, just as he said. A dilapidated sign on the side bore the legend 'Liberian Institute for Biomedical Research'.

It sent chills down my spine.

220

Thirty-two

P ETER HOOTED FOR SOMEONE TO open the gate. A security guard walked over and when we explained our business, he told us there were no longer any chimps on the premises.

However, he let us in and Peter drove down the driveway where it split into two pathways.

Greeting us was a dilapidated carving of a rather strange looking chimp. To the left was a big empty building and Mark got out to peer through the window.

There was no one inside. Mark returned to the car, telling Peter to take the other track. A little farther along we saw some empty cages surrounded by a fence. Missy was staring out the window, blissfully unaware of her surroundings, while I was uncomfortably aware that we were on a site where hundreds of medical experiments had been done on her species.

A staff member saw our car and came over to ask what we wanted.

Mark said we were looking for Joseph Thomas. We were told that he was on his way back from Marshall Island, or Monkey Island as it is more commonly called, and would be arriving in about 10 minutes. If we waited, we could speak to him.

Mark then asked the man where the chimpanzees were being kept. He shook his head. Not here, he said. They were all on the island.

Mark rephrased, "No, not the island animals. I mean the chimpanzees in the cages here. Where are they?"

"There aren't any chimpanzees here," the staff member repeated. "All are now on Marshall Island."

With that the man offered to show Mark where the chimps had once been kept. Just as we were told, the few cages that had not been dissembled were empty. In other words, we now knew for an absolute certainty that Liberia officially had no place for orphaned chimps to be sheltered.

The laboratory, where we were waiting for Mr. Thomas, had started up in 1975 when the New York-based Blood Center signed a contract with the Liberian Biomedical Research Center to do testing on chimpanzees, including studies which led to the development of a low-cost Hepatitis B vaccine.

After undergoing tests, the chimps were released on Marshall Island, which is actually a group of six islands, just

222

off Liberia's coastline. They could not be returned to the jungles as they had been subjected to barrages of laboratory experiments, which could infect wild chimps. Also, most of the chimps wouldn't know how to survive in the wild because they were taken away from their mothers when they were just babies. As chimps can't swim, there was no risk of the laboratory animals escaping from Marshall Island, so it is now a permanent quarantine area for them.

A car drove up a few minutes later. A Liberian man got out and introduced himself. This was the legendary Joseph Thomas, who for 37 years has looked after the laboratory animals. A friendly-faced man with frizzed gray hair, he probably knows more about chimps than anyone else in Liberia and had developed a strong bond with the animals on the islands.

Mark cut to the chase, "Where are the orphaned chimps? We were told they are kept here."

Mr. Thomas shook his head. There were no orphaned chimps in the old laboratory buildings. He stressed that the only chimps still in their care were those living on Marshall Island. Most of the cages have since been dismantled and he confirmed what we now already knew – that there was no official sanctuary or reserve in Liberia that could take care of Missy.

Mark then asked if Mr. Thomas personally would be able to look after Missy for a few months while we sorted things out from South Africa. He looked at Missy with much compassion before he sadly shook his head.

"I'm afraid not. I don't have the time. Taking care of the chimps at Marshall Island is a full time job."

We knew what he meant. Every day of the week he had to go out to the islands, visiting three islands each alternate day in a motorboat to feed the 66 or so chimpanzees that would otherwise starve. He just didn't have the capacity to cater or care for any more.

We thanked Mr. Thomas, not just for taking the time to speak to us, but for his dedicated work with the chimpanzees. I instinctively knew how deep that devotion was. I felt that same for Missy.

It was already Saturday. The clock was ticking relentless towards our departure date and we were still in a seemingly impossible situation.

The next day it was back to the farm again. Mark and I were tired of travelling along the awful road, but the reality was that we had nowhere else to go where Missy would not be in potential danger.

However, this too was becoming problematic as our visits to the farm were also getting increasingly restrictive. We couldn't take her to the restaurant and if I needed to go to the restroom I had to leave Missy with Mark.

Sometimes she was calm, but most of the time she screamed blue murder when I left, even though it was only for a few minutes. This was always a worry as it could have attracted unwanted attention if other guests were nearby.

With only the golf course, Juliet's sauna-like apartment, or the car as options where we could spend the day, it was an exhausting, draining and tedious time for both of us.

There was no other choice. So Mark and I just soldiered on.

Thirty-three

O N MONDAY MORNING ANNIE told us that she could only babysit until Friday that week as her sister was going back home at the weekend.

This was a bit of a blow as the sister looked after Annie's children while she babysat Missy. But it wasn't an insurmountable problem as we had Juliet's apartment, even though there still was no running water or electricity. Or any indication that there ever would be.

Then two days later I got an email from a man called Bassel Abifaraj who had read about our plight on the website. He managed a compound of homes in Congo Town, and knowing that Missy could not possibly be an Ebola risk, he offered us a place to stay.

It sounded great, so Peter drove Missy and I to meet the caretaker and look around.

It was better than I had dared to hope. Far better. The compound had five spacious houses equipped with three bedrooms and two bathrooms. The buildings were separated by decent size gardens which even had grass, unusual for Liberian homes.

But best of all, the homes all had power and running water. My only concern was how much it would cost.

First I let Mark know that it was the perfect place for us, then I phoned Bassel, saying I really liked the house, but needed to know what the rent would be.

Our savings were our only income at that time, but Mark never hesitated. He never questioned and never complained about the rocketing expenses mounting up in looking after Missy. He was fantastic – an absolute tower of strength in these dark days.

Bassel said he would only charge for the use of the generator. I was elated and overwhelmed by his generosity.

On Friday morning Peter dropped me and Missy off at our new home. It was on the main road through Congo Town, about a 20-minute drive from Ocean View. The car was loaded with food, linen, clothes, and all of Missy's belongings. The compound caretaker met me at the house to give me the keys.

I could hardly believe our good fortune. As soon as I had everything unpacked, I took Missy onto the grass. She held my hand and ran up and down, shrieking with delight.

At the edge of the garden was a tiny tree, which Missy headed straight for and started swinging on the branches. Even though she was tiny, she was still strong enough to snap them. Not wanting to destroy the tree on our first day – which would really be abusing our hospitality – I picked her up and we went for a walk.

The rest of the day Missy and I spent either resting inside or playing outside. It was a real feeling of freedom to wander around in the garden without worrying about being seen or reported by snooping neighbors.

Then an expat from Kenya heard about Missy. He offered to take care of her for a few months while we sorted out everything in South Africa. I phoned him, and he said that he lived in a one-bedroom apartment, but worked from home.

That seemed promising as he would be with her all day. But I explained that looking after Missy was a full time job. Going out anywhere with her would be nearly impossible with the current Ebola hysteria. He would have to watch her every move.

The truth is that looking after a baby chimp is not a leisurely chore under any circumstances. But in Liberia, with a deadly virus stalking the land and chimps thought to be carriers, it was downright dangerous.

I wanted to make that absolutely clear to anyone volunteering to take Missy in, and I obviously did so quite vividly in this case. For after making arrangements to meet me, he never pitched up.

So that was that – another door closed.

However, he did have the decency to call me back a couple of days later saying that perhaps it was too much of a responsibility for him. He also said he was now considering leaving the country himself due to the Ebola threat.

This was fairly typical among the expats. More and more were returning home as the Ebola crisis showed no sign of abating.

Many foreign companies also didn't want to risk their expat employees' health, so they sent them back to their native countries to wait until the epidemic passed.

Thirty-four

WE WERE FAST APPROACHING our last few weeks in Liberia. And we still had no one to look after Missy, or a place where she could go to.

This played havoc with my state of mind and I was becoming more and more anxious. I had no idea of what I was going to do. All I did know was that there was no way that I was going to run off and leave her.

The guilt that she was about to lose another 'mother' was constantly on my mind. The other option, having her euthanized before we left – as the Zambian vet had suggested – was something I also couldn't bear to think about. Mark and I hadn't discussed it further since that phone call to the Zambian vet.

But a spark of optimism still burned. Somehow I believed in my heart, if not my head, that against all odds we would still pull it off. That we would have a miracle ending.

On Monday morning Mark and I went to Bassel's office to thank him personally for letting us stay at his compound. Meeting him in the flesh confirmed what a decent and good man he was, just as I had imagined him to be while speaking on the phone. He also was thrilled to meet Missy, who reciprocated by being on her best behavior.

On the way back I stopped off in Congo Town on the off-chance that Etag had any good news for us. She shook her head sadly.

That evening I suggested to Mark that perhaps I should stay a little longer in Liberia until everything was sorted. Mark did not like that at all.

"You won't have a car. What if you get sick? You are so wrecked already. Ebola is getting out of hand. What if you don't find a solution? You will not cope on your own."

He was right. I couldn't deny that I was in bad shape emotionally, and I also recoiled at the thought of Mark not being with me.

But what to do about Missy?

"No one can pass judgement on you," said Mark. "You have sacrificed everything to take care of her, so you are the one person who knows what is best."

He looked at me for a long while before continuing. I could see he was choosing his words carefully. His expression was sad.

"Remember your first instinct when we first saw her? Remember you saying you believed that she would be better off with her real mother?"

He continued looking gently at me as I digested his words. He was saying as softly and tactfully as he could that euthanasia may be the only option left. If we didn't find somewhere suitable for her to stay, her life would be an absolute misery in any event.

"I can't do it," I said. "I simply can't. Maybe she will be okay for a few months here until Ebola blows over?"

I was painfully aware that I was saying that more out of blind hope than conviction. The reality was that there was nowhere in Liberia for Missy to stay.

"I wish we could just smuggle her out to the sanctuary in Guinea," I said, on the verge of tears. "I wish we could just put her in a car and somehow get her out of Liberia."

It came out of the blue. Mark was watching me, a quizzical expression on his face.

"Are you serious?"

I nodded.

This unlocked a whole new scenario – something we had not openly considered previously. Every option we were exploring had been through government channels and getting official approval.

But what if there was another option? One we hadn't thought of before? What if we just put her in a car and smuggled her out?

Guinea was part of West Africa, so Ebola was not something alien as it was with other countries. In fact, the current epidemic had actually started in Guinea, and border closures were not as rigidly enforced.

"I'm deadly serious. Why can't we drive Missy to the chimp sanctuary in Guinea? Take our chances with that?"

Without saying another word Mark picked up the phone and dialed the sanctuary manager, a remarkable woman called Estelle Raballand.

The Centre de Conservation pour Chimpanzés, or Chimpanzee Conservation Center (CCC), is the only chimp sanctuary in Guinea. It's located in the Parc National du Haut Niger, and rehabilitates many rescued chimpanzees. Most chimps cared for there have been confiscated from despicable wild animal traders, or those like Missy who have been orphaned by bushmeat hunters.

Estelle has been the director of the CCC since 1999 and has worked with chimpanzees since 1994 in four different countries. She was in the Guinea capital Conakry when Mark phoned and there was a bad connection, so they made arrangements to talk on Skype the following day.

I didn't get much sleep that night with my mounting excitement.

Maybe, just maybe, the miracle I had hoped for would happen.

Thirty-five

I WOKE THE NEXT DAY with mounting anticipation and couldn't wait for the Skype conversation between Mark and Estelle to start.

Estelle was totally dedicated to the chimps in her care and is an absolutely exceptional person. Animals in general and chimpanzees in particular are her life.

Estelle already knew about Missy. She explained that the sanctuary can't accept chimps directly from another country. In fact, they could only accept chimps that have been confiscated by the Guinean authorities.

Fortunately, with her compassion and total devotion to saving chimpanzees she said she would do whatever she could to help us. She said she would let us know more the next day as, apart from all else, she also needed the approval of the board of directors.

True to her word, when Mark spoke with her again, things were looking much better. I soon realized why she is such a powerful personality in the animal rescue and rehabilitation world.

Firstly, the good news was that the board of directors had agreed to take in Missy because of the exceptional circumstances.

But there was one catch – the 'confiscation'. As Estelle mentioned the day before, Missy would still have to be 'confiscated' and handed over to the Guinean authorities. A fee to care of $1,000 was requested. Even though they knew that we were not guilty of buying Missy, it was still strict protocol.

I was ecstatic. Mark immediately agreed to their terms and he was more than willing to pay the confiscation fee.

The next hurdle was a massive one. How could we get Missy over the border to Guinea and past Liberian customs?

Mark spoke to an expat friend to find out if they could transport her by helicopter. They could, but only as far as the Liberian border. There was no way that they could legally fly into Guinea.

It was now clear to us that the only way to get Missy into Guinea was to cross the border by vehicle along some of the worst roads in the world.

For that we needed a serious off-road 4x4 as well as some human 'muscle', a man who would not be intimidated by the numerous military roadblocks, who could 'persuade' custom's officials to perhaps look in the other direction if necessary, and generally charm or bulldoze his way through.

We had the perfect man for the job. My bodyguard Pebbles, the man who blocked anyone pestering me when I went to the Waterfront Market.

Mark phoned Pebbles and got straight to the point.

"I need a favor, my friend. We have a baby chimpanzee that needs to be taken to a sanctuary in Guinea. We will have most of the necessary paperwork, but it may not be easy. Would you be able to do that for us?"

Pebbles said he was sure he could help.

He arrived at the compound the following day to discuss tactics with Mark. We told him Missy's story and where she would need to go. Mark said that officials would be informed about the exceptional circumstances regarding Missy's plight and with the necessary documents, Pebbles should not – fingers crossed – encounter too many problems.

Pebbles agreed to take her. Like any Liberian, he knew that 'should not' encounter problems with officialdom did not mean 'would not'. We had no doubt he was the right man for the job.

I originally wanted to go with him, but a white face at the border deep in the jungle would spark too much attention. It could put everyone in jeopardy.

Consequently, Mark decided it would be better that both he and I stay behind. He was right. We needed this operation to be as far under the radar as possible.

Pebbles got hold of a friend, Samuel, who would help with the long and extremely arduous drive along sometimes barely passable mud tracks. Samuel could also speak French, which is widely used in Guinea. That alone was a substantial added bonus.

Mark and Pebbles then discussed payment for the mission and where to hire a sturdy 4x4 vehicle.

Also in on the plan was Estelle, and she and Mark were in constant contact as they worked out the best route into Guinea.

All in all, it would be a five-day journey: two days to Faranah, the closest Guinean town to the CCC sanctuary, another day to the sanctuary and back to Faranah, and then two days returning to Monrovia.

They would leave on Thursday morning.

The realization that I only had three more nights with Missy was bittersweet. I was ecstatic that she would be going to an outstanding sanctuary, but dreading the absolute finality of having to say goodbye forever. Also, the three-day trip with two strangers would be traumatic for her.

Mark contacted Mr. Francisco, the Department of Agriculture official who had tried to help us in the past, and spent most of the following day organizing the necessary documents.

Mark and Pebbles met again later in the day, going through maps, routes, and covering every miniscule detail of the trip. Both are former soldiers and planned the trip with military precision. They even worked out an alternative route if everything went up in smoke. Plan B involved crossing the Lofa River into Guinea on a raft able to float the 4x4 if border post officials refused to let them through, or if the roads became too risky.

I messaged Phoebe and all of our supporters to tell them that there would be a farewell get-together on Wednesday evening for Missy at the Congo Town house.

Mark and I decided it would be best not to tell anyone, with the exception of Phoebe, where Missy was going until she had arrived safely at the sanctuary. Phoebe would be in on the plan as she had rescued numerous animals in Africa before. She even had a travelling cage, which she offered to lend us for the trip. We accepted gratefully.

On Wednesday, Peter went to the supermarket to get extra milk, fruit, antibacterial soap for Missy and stocked up with food and loads of water for Pebbles and Samuel.

I called Etag to see if she had a natural sedative to relax Missy for the trip. She didn't, so I stopped at the pharmacy to ask what they had to calm a baby, figuring that would also work for a small chimp.

Mark then phoned John to tell him that Missy would be leaving the next day and asked him to make an exception for her to stay at Ocean View on her last night.

To our eternal relief, John agreed, but said we must keep her hidden in the apartment.

Adding to all the frenetic buzz, the container for our belongings was arriving on the same day that Missy left and we needed to be at the compound to load it up for South Africa. Mark and I had not yet packed a single item.

Phoebe pitched up at the compound in the late afternoon. She had bought some snacks for Missy and the travelling cage with a thick comfortable blanket. We cushioned the cage with the blanket.

Without Mogli for comfort, Phoebe brought her own fluffy toy called Tigger so that Missy would have something to cuddle during the trip. Phoebe had owned Tigger for years. It always travelled with her and was a hugely sentimental possession. I asked if she was sure, not being able to guarantee Tigger's return.

"Missy will need Tigger far more than I will," was Phoebe's magnificent response.

Phoebe's generosity was no surprise with her many acts of helping animals in need and her generosity with donations to help various organizations.

She picked up Tigger and showed the fluffy toy to Missy, who was a little scared at first. So we left Tigger on the couch for her to get used to it.

A little later Missy grew curious and went to 'make friends'. After some initial reluctance she picked Tigger up.

Phoebe then showed Missy her treats for the trip and we told her about the beautiful place she was going to.

Just before other guests arrived I washed Missy's hands with antibacterial soap. She loved the attention. It was as if she knew the party was in her honor. It was an emotional goodbye, but also a celebration that she was going to a beautiful new home.

My heart had already started palpitating with the dreaded thought of saying goodbye the next day.

When we arrived back at Ocean View it was past Missy's bedtime. I went to the bedroom to lie down with her until she fell asleep. This was the last time I would have her sleep with me. She soon drifted off and I watched her for a while.

Then very gently I lifted her arm off me. I had to go and pack.

However, my heart was not in it. I kept going back into the bedroom to look in on Missy.

"Crocodile, go to bed," said Mark. "Annie and Peter will help us and we'll finish packing as quickly as we can tomorrow."

I climbed into bed and just watched Missy sleeping for most of the night. At one stage she woke up and I went to get her some milk.

It was the last time I would ever do that.

Thirty-six

MISSY WOKE HAPPY AS ALWAYS on our final morning together, blissfully unaware that we would never see each other again.

Even though I knew she was going to a beautiful place, I ached at the thought of the last goodbye. I knew the next few days were going to be traumatic for her.

My heart was now pounding like a freight train; my body had gone into mild shock from all the anxiety. I began to shake and fumbled with even the simplest of tasks.

The doorbell rang. It was Pebbles. Missy greeted him and he reciprocated with a tender pat on her back. It did my heart good to see that. Pebbles seemed to care for her.

He sat on the couch next to Missy while he and Mark went through the final paperwork and the route they would take to get to the border. I then gave Missy some of the natural calming sedative, measuring less than what was recommended for her weight.

While they were doing that, Missy left my arm and moved towards Pebbles. He gave her another gentle rub on her back and said a few words to her. They were definitely bonding, and I cannot put into words how relieved I was.

When the paperwork was done, I showed Pebbles how to fill Missy's bottle, the right mix of milk powder and water, and how to change her diaper.

I put an extra towel, my throw that Missy was familiar with, and Tigger into the cage. I then gave Pebbles my camera to take some photos of the trip for me.

At 10 o'clock I heard a car arrive. It was Samuel.

My panic increased. The car, to me, did not sound in good mechanical condition.

I turned to Mark. "Foxy, did you hear noises coming from the car? How it struggled to start? What if they get stuck?"

Mark and Annie both reassured me it was fine and I should calm down.

"How do you know?" I barked at them.

By now my legs were weak and I was trembling. Annie and Pebbles packed the car. They put the traveling cage on the backseat and left the door open.

The sight of the cage in the car again set off my anxiety at the thought of how stressful the separation and the trip would be for Missy. We had to put her in the cage in case she tried to bite Pebbles in her panic.

Samuel started the car. There was just an ominous 'click'. He turned the key again.

Nothing.

I was beside myself. I hissed at Mark, "They will get stuck!"

After a couple more attempts, Samuel lifted the bonnet.

It was a simple problem. The battery was dead.

Mark asked Peter to take Pebbles and Samuel into town to buy another one. They returned an hour later and I managed to calm down a little, most relieved that the car was now working.

It was time to say goodbye. I told Mark that he would have to put Missy in the cage as I couldn't do it. With tears streaming down my face I kissed and hugged her.

"Bye my precious girly. I will think of you every minute of every day."

I sniffed and said the last words I would ever say to her, "You are going to be with your own kind."

I watched through blurred eyes as Mark placed her in the cage. He said goodbye and closed the door. I heard her screaming as the car drove out the compound, a sound that tore through me and will be with me for the rest of my life.

I was absolutely broken that I couldn't console her, wishing she understood she was going to a wonderful place. Wishing she would understand that we were doing the best we could for her.

Mark walked inside to give me a hug. Even though I knew she had never belonged to me, my heart didn't agree.

The car turned onto the street as it left the compound. I could no longer see it.

Missy was gone.

Thirty-Seven

MARK WAS IN CELL PHONE CONTACT with Pebbles as much as possible during the hazardous trip.

He had bought Pebbles plenty of airtime so we could get regular updates, although in some areas there was no network reception.

Whenever that happened, my heart was in my mouth and no matter how hard I tried, I always imagined the worst. Had they broken down? Were soldiers harassing them at roadblocks? Had Missy been confiscated by officials?

The Lofa border area between Guinea and Liberia was the epicenter of the Ebola outbreak and so having a chimp in a car was a nerve-wracking and risky drive.

Pebbles, with his imposing presence, and Samuel were perfect candidates to take her. But even so, I was worried for their safety as well as Missy's.

Fortunately, packing up all our belongings to go back to South Africa gave me something to do on that bitter-sweet day. With Missy's long trip and the seemingly endless wait to find out if she would get to the sanctuary safely, it was a much-needed distraction.

Even so, I felt as though I was missing a vital appendage. Missy had been clinging almost constantly to my side for five months. That had been my default pose; a baby chimp glued to my hip.

So it was not just an emotional upheaval – it was a raw, physical loss. She possessed a chunk of my heart. A chunk that I knew would never grow back the same again.

The first leg of the trip was about 11 hours to get to Voinjama, the capital city of Lofa County and close to the border with Guinea.

When they arrived, Pebbles called to say they had been stopped at several checkpoints but had managed to talk their way through.

They booked into at a motel for the night. Although exhausted, they still had to think on their feet while negotiating their way out of a major potential problem when the motel managed refused to allow Missy inside.

Eventually, more money changed hands, and suddenly Missy was welcome.

Pebbles said Missy was fine and that she had slept a lot on the way. I was pleased to hear that she was eager to have her milk and couldn't help but chuckle at the thought of a hulking, muscle-bound African man changing her diaper.

I reminded Pebbles to wash Missy's hands with antibacterial soap and not to let her touch anyone. He assured me that was being taken care of.

The following morning, Pebbles, Samuel and Missy left the motel early and arrived at the border at around nine.

The anticipation of finding out if they had got through to Guinea was absolutely unbearable for me. Time dragged and I was constantly checking the clock. This was potentially the riskiest part of the trip. Would the border guards, who are often a law unto themselves, allow Missy through?

The irony was that the fear of Ebola and the mistaken belief that a chimp was a carrier of the virus could actually lessen the risk of Missy being confiscated. Ignorance was particularly rife in the back country, and the border guards were likely to be extremely fearful of having any contact with her. They certainly were not going to pick her up.

At least, that was what I hoped.

At last Pebbles called Mark to say that they had crossed the border. As expected, the Liberian authorities had given him and Samuel a hard time before allowing them through. Despite the papers from the Department of Agriculture, it took a lot of convincing and, of course, a 'fee' (bribe to you and me) to get them to lift the boom barrier into Guinea.

Conversely, getting though on the Guinean side was plain sailing. The guards checked that their papers were in order and then waived them through.

Pebbles and Samuel left the border at about 11 a.m. and then it was another grueling nine hours to Faranah, where they and Missy spent the night.

The next day three volunteers from the Chimpanzee Conservation Centre, which is about 80km from Faranah, arrived in town to pick up supplies. Estelle had come from Conakry to be in Faranah as well to bring Missy back to the CCC on Sunday.

As we had previously arranged, Pebbles and Samuel met Estelle. They paid the care fee that Mark had given them – although $800 instead of the $1,000 agreed on as Pebbles had had to spend an extra $200 on unforeseen bribes.

Missy was now legally in Guinea. At last, she was on the threshold of a new life; a life where she would never be hunted for bushmeat, sold as a pet to be abused, or treated as a pariah due to appalling ignorance.

The Parc National du Haut Niger where the CCC is situated is in an extremely isolated part of Guinea. Part of the Niger River runs through it and the only road from Faranah consists of little more than rutted dirt tracks. So although it is not that far as the crow flies, the journey takes at least five hours.

The initial plan was that Pebbles and Samuel would follow the volunteers to the sanctuary to spread the load of passengers. But the people from the CCC said they didn't think Pebbles' hired 4x4 would make it through the rugged terrain. So there was no point in them tagging along.

Their mission now admirably accomplished, Pebbles and Samuel started the two-day grind back to Liberia.

That night Missy slept with her new caretakers in Faranah. The next day she arrived at her new home, the CCC.

It had been a long, heart-wrenching journey for all of us. From the moment I laid eyes on Missy at Jack and Dorothy's farm, to the tearful farewell as we were packing up to leave for South Africa, for me it had been the ultimate rollercoaster ride. I don't think there will ever be anything else to equal it in my life.

But we had won. Despite everything thrown at us; the bureaucracy, the fear, the ignorance and, of course, Ebola, Mark and I had managed to save Missy's life.

She was now in a place she belonged.

She was with her own kind.

Epilogue

A FEW DAYS AFTER MISSY HAD settled into her new home, we arrived back in South Africa with no car and no job.

In fact, our only asset of any note was a small one-bedroom apartment, which we decided to completely gut and renovate.

While this was happening, we stayed with Mark's mother for a few weeks until the building work was completed.

Mark got a job about a month later, while I resumed doing pet grooming work. Mark's new job was way below his skills level and he was really punching below his weight. But as jobs for white men are scarce in South Africa with Black Economic Empowerment policies now entrenched in law, he had to take what he could.

While pet grooming, I also started working on getting an electronic greeting card website for veterinary practices up and running, which became my new career.

We also kept in regular contact with our friends in Liberia. By now word was out on how we had managed to slip Missy out of the country and get her into a world class sanctuary.

One delightful snippet of news was that Mogli was found by a staff member at the Libassa Ecolodge. Perhaps it will be of comfort to another orphan one day – just as it had to Missy. I truly hope so.

Etag also called us to see if we could help with another Liberian chimp, a three-year-old called Lily that was in terrible shape. Lily spent her days locked in a tiny cage, just rocking back and forth in miserable isolation and vulnerable to abuse.

Etag wanted to know if we could find her a sanctuary as we had done with Missy.

At about the same time Phoebe heard about a baby chimp named Jack that was permanently tied up to a rusted car behind a police station. He had been tied to the car for months. The poor youngster's diet was occasional fruit, and apparently beer but no milk.

Mark had also been in regular contact with some of his former staff to see how they were coping with the Ebola outbreak after we left. Sadly, one had been a victim and died. Mark also learned that a lot of pet chimps were killed during the epidemic as well.

With the help of a welfare organization initiated by Phoebe called Ispare (International Sammy Project for Animal Rescue and Education) and the Libassa Ecolodge, the first and only wildlife sanctuary in Liberia, both Lily, renamed

Sweet Pea and Jack now named Guey (Kru and Grebo words for chimp) were taken to the Libassa Eco Lodge where they were well taken care of in spacious cages.

Sweet Pea and Guey, together with five other orphans, have now been moved to a temporary sanctuary set up at the Liberian Institute for Biomedical research (LIBR) – the animal and medical analysis center where we met Joseph Thomas – and are being well cared for.

Sadly, we also learned that funding for the chimps on Marshall Island had dried up with the New York Blood Center terminating financial support for the chimps.

As a result, the islands are under the administration of LIBR, which is itself struggling to survive due to lack of funding. The New York Blood Center is an organization that has generated hundreds of millions of dollars from experiments done on Liberian chimps. It is of extreme concern to animal lovers that the laboratory chimps were deliberately infected with the Hepatitis B virus, and then abandoned by the NYBC.

If it wasn't for devoted Samaritans as well as the dedicated staff who had been caring for the animals for so many years, the chimps on the islands would have starved to death or died from dehydration.

At the moment the Humane Society of the United States are providing funds with donations from the public. There is currently a married couple, Jenny and Jim Desmond living in Liberia and caring for the chimps with the help of the long-time loyal caregivers. An organization called Liberia Chimpanzee Rescue, which Jenny, and Jim and a team of approximately 30 people run with the support of GoFundMe campaign was launched. They work closely with the FDA.

The positive news for the chimps in Liberia is a new Wildlife Bill has been passed, and Liberia has had their first ever arrest of two chimp traffickers. The sale of wildlife species, wildlife as pets or food is now prohibited. This is a major step in the right direction.

Meanwhile, back in South Africa, Mark and I got married. He is my absolute rock. With Missy, I may have provided the love and emotional support, but everything else – from buying diapers to paying the administration fees – came out of Mark's pocket. We were also unemployed at the time, so no money was coming in. Yet not once did Mark quibble, and not once did he weaken. I don't think he is capable of weakening.

Liberia certainly showed us that as a couple we are able to endure both good and bad times – in spades!

However, back in South Africa we became increasingly despondent over Mark getting a decent job. Mark has many business contacts who would have loved to have him work for them, but couldn't do so as they were legally barred from hiring whites.

We then had a chance to get a Green Card to the United States, so we put our apartment on the market and planned to start a new life in Texas. With the immigration legalities, we decided it would be easier to arrive as a married couple so we had an informal, small wedding in June 2015.

However, soon afterwards Mark got an offer to work in Mozambique, so we chose to move there instead.

We have recently moved back to South Africa and are settling in a little community adjacent to the Kruger National Park, where we are surrounded by some of the less-dangerous wild animals. It is our dream place to live, waking up to the sounds of the birds and animals and part of the Crocodile River and a piece of the Kruger National Park as our view. It is about an hour and a half away from Chimp Eden.

Whatever the future brings, I know that I will always work with animals. I will never stop caring for them and being their voice.

It's a two-way process. I get as much from animals as I give to them. Probably even more so. The lessons I learnt from Missy were invaluable. In her own way, she taught me so much.

I learnt that helping just one animal may not save the planet but it can change its life and your life by inspiring you to do more. If one animal lover rescued or sponsored just one endangered animal to be cared for by a reputable sanctuary, the world would be a far better place for all creatures that call this planet home.

We can all help in many other ways such as buying smarter – stop buying environmentally harmful products like unsustainable palm oil products; recycling; not supporting circuses or tourist attractions that exploit and abuse animals; not buying greeting cards with chimps dressed up as humans. Or even better, instead of buying gifts rather donate to a sanctuary on behalf of someone as a gift; or include a reputable animal sanctuary in your Will.

The journey also taught me to accept who I am, warts and all. To accept my vulnerabilities and embrace my

255

strengths. There will always be someone more brave, more devoted, more educated. But at the same time, it gave me unyielding determination to fight even harder for those creatures dying in their millions.

I am not so naïve to believe that the world will one day magically become a better place for those creatures being massacred daily in the barbaric bushmeat trade. I also understand that many involved in bushmeat hunting in the West African rainforests do so for their own survival.

But there has to be another way. Or else there will be no animals left in the African jungles.

I have no glib answers, but there are some things ordinary people like you and I can do to improve the lives of these critically endangered creatures. In fact, there are already steps in place.

For example, we should stand up in our millions and demand that CITES (The Convention on International Trade in Endangered Species of Wild Fauna and Flora) be vigorously enforced. There are still numerous loopholes and corrupt officials can easily issue permits for illegal animal trading. Those officials must be ruthlessly weeded out.

We also need to focus on massive education and countries that have no animal rights need to be put under pressure to change their ways and their laws for animal rights.

For example, orphaned chimps are still being illegally smuggled into China for the entertainment industry there. They are kept as pets, dressed up and treated like children.

The problem is that they – like abused children – grow up to be extremely aggressive adults and as a consequence are either killed or thrown into cages. They will never be able to be re-introduced back to the wild, and those that are lucky enough to go to a reputable sanctuary, almost always don't know how to interact with the other chimps.

In other countries, such as the United Arab Emirates, it's become a status symbol to have exotic animals as pets. This too, obviously must stop.

But it only will if the glare of publicity is shone incessantly on the perpetrators. And the next generation must be taught in no uncertain manner that animals are not solely on this planet either to eat or abuse, or for our entertainment.

But back to Missy.

Missy has thrived at Chimpanzee Conservation Center. Upon her arrival she had round the clock care with two volunteer caregivers in her new forest environment. She settled down quite quickly with her new caregivers who gave her lots of tickles and love. The first few months she was in quarantine. From early on she was introduced to learning chimp ways and chimp etiquette.

Missy is currently in the babies group with two other orphans, Noel and Hawa. Noel was rescued from the pet trade and Hawa from the bushmeat trade.

Their days are spent with a volunteer and caregiver. At 8 a.m until noon they spend their day in the forest learning the necessary skills to survive. They are taught vital skills in the bush like climbing trees and discovering wild food.

At noon they go back to their sleeping quarters for a midday rest. At 3 p.m they go back to the forest until 6pm when they are fed their last meal and then go to bed.

They are fed four times a day: 7.30 a.m., midday, 3 p.m. and then at 6 p.m. They receive milk at 7.30 a.m., midday and at 6 p.m.

Missy at first slept at night with Noel, but he became very annoying, so they moved her in with Hawa.

Missy and her babies' group were introduced to the juvenile group last July. It takes time to introduce the chimps into a new group, but Missy integrated very well as the baby of the group.

The older chimps are very good with her, although Missy can be nasty with Leonie who used to be the baby of the group. Leonie came from Sierra Leone in 2011. She had a bullet in her brain, resulting her in being semi- paralyzed. She had brain surgery in 2012 which saved her life.

With the outstanding care at Chimpanzee Conservation Center, Missy's personality has started to show more and more.

She has demonstrated a lot of natural behavior which is imperative for her future with other chimps. She still loves interacting with her human caregivers and is quite the princess.

Even with the happy ending that Missy deserved, no sanctuary could replace her family, no act of love or care can undo the tragedy her and her family faced on the day the hunters killed her mother and other family members.

258

The brutal killing that she witnessed and then being yanked from her from her dead mother's body to be sold. Her family is probably a faded memory, but it was her birthright to live in the forests with her kind.

Above all, rescuing Missy, showed me that we can never give up speaking for those who cannot speak for themselves.

It's a lesson I'll take with me to the grave.

The End

Acknowledgements

ON THE UNFORGETTABLE day that I first met Missy, little did I know how it would change my life. The journey in getting her to a safe haven to be with her kind showed me the good and bad in human kind.

The goodness is the memory that remains profound and engraved in my heart, where there is a chunk of gratitude for so much kindness and meeting beautiful souls.

The first thank you is to Mark, my husband, my clichéd other half for the financial and emotional support and for enduring my emotional roller coaster ride. You gave me encouragement to finish writing the book when I doubted myself. You always lift me up, make me feel braver, make me laugh, and help me to see things positively, always shining the spotlight on hope.

To Phillip Cronje, my friend from Chimp Eden, a heartfelt thank you for your professional advice and encouragement to write the book for the chimps when I felt unworthy compared to so many more brave and devoted animal warriors. How lucky am I to have become friends with one of my heroes! I hope that you write a book about your own hair-raising chimp rescues. Only by getting to know you have I learned how much you have done for chimpanzees. A true testament to your humble personality. Thank you for all the effort you put into trying to get Missy into Chimp Eden, and even after the ban on her entry because of Ebola you were there with us every step of the way. Thank you for all that you do for the chimps at Chimp Eden and your voice and help for other animals in need of help or a voice.

Thank you Phoebe McKinney for your kindness and generosity, your passion for animals is contagious.

Thank you Etag (Etagegnehu D Belayneh), for caring for all the animals that come your way in Liberia. You went out of your way to help Missy and me. I will never forget your kindness. You are a beautiful human being.

Thank you to all my friends and family, especially my cousin Robyn Kapral for your help and words of support.

Thank you to the many kind people, too many to mention, for your support and help.

To Annie and Bettie, thank you for babysitting and caring for Missy, especially Annie for taking care of her when no one else would. Thank you for standing by her and me during the Ebola panic.

Thank you Lisa Viau Antoune and Rudolph Antoune for giving Missy and me a place to stay in your piece of paradise – especially because it is my favorite place in Liberia. How proud you must be of your little sanctuary you built for the animals that were rescued and now have a place to be cared for.

Thank you Bassel Abifaraj and Juliet Matthews for your wonderful generosity in giving us safe places to stay at no charge.

Thank you Michael Jedig Jensen and Emily Tarr for taking some beautiful photographs of Missy for me to cherish and for providing a beautiful photo for the cover of the book.

Thank you to Pebbles and Samuel for taking a very risky drive under very stressful and dangerous roads to Guinea. I salute your bravery.

Thank you to Karl Ammann for information and your lifelong dedication in exposing and sharing the terrible realities of the bushmeat trade.

Thank you to my twin sister Sandra Viljoen, my other-other half, for your support, unmatched empathy and huge heart for animals.

Thank you to Mark's mom Arlene Fox, for reading all the updated versions and your kind inspiration to carry on.

A giant-sized, heartfelt thank you to Estelle Raballand and Chimpanzee Conservation Center for your outstanding devotion for all the chimps in your care. Thank you for giving Missy the miracle happy ending we desperately needed during a very challenging time with the Ebola outbreak. Even though I have never had the privilege of meeting you Estelle, I know you are a humble animal warrior champion. A formidable, fearless woman fighting for the survival of chimpanzees, working non-stop, not for credit or praise, but for making every chimpanzee you can have a better life. I will quote your use of the word, chimpian; you are a humble chimpian.

To my father: Dad even though you passed away so young, there is not a day that goes by that I think of you. Thank you for instilling my love of animals and for teaching me to speak for them.

Thank you Tami Rose for your talented, creative input in designing the front and back cover.

Thank you to Graham Spence for co-authoring my book. I can still hardly believe such an inspiring bestselling, published author co-authored my book. Plus, you gave me so much extra help with everything from the cover to all the nitty-gritties of writing a book.

Lastly, thank you to all the reputable sanctuaries without whom the chimps would not have had a second chance. The unseen heroes who work tirelessly to care for and save the chimps in their care.

To all the animal lovers, every little bit of help for animals no matter how small will make a difference. The enormity of the challenges can be overwhelming but we must never give up helping.

I have created a Facebook page with details for Missy and her chimp friends called 'For Missy and her chimp friends'.

Chimpanzee Conservation Center -www.projetprimates.com

Chimp Eden - www.chimpeden.com

About the author:

Gail Gillespie Fox was born in South Africa. She grew up with three dogs that were the foundation of her love of animals. Her identical twin sister and her always dreamed of working with animals one day. Her first job was working at a music company, but while many people dream of working in the music industry her passion remained to work with animals. While working at a music company she got a shih tzu puppy who stole her heart and was the catapult in a new career.

For 18 years she ran her own dog grooming business, a career she loved with all her heart.

She lives with her husband Mark in Mpumalanga, South Africa.

Her name is Missy